THIS BOOK

BELONGS TO

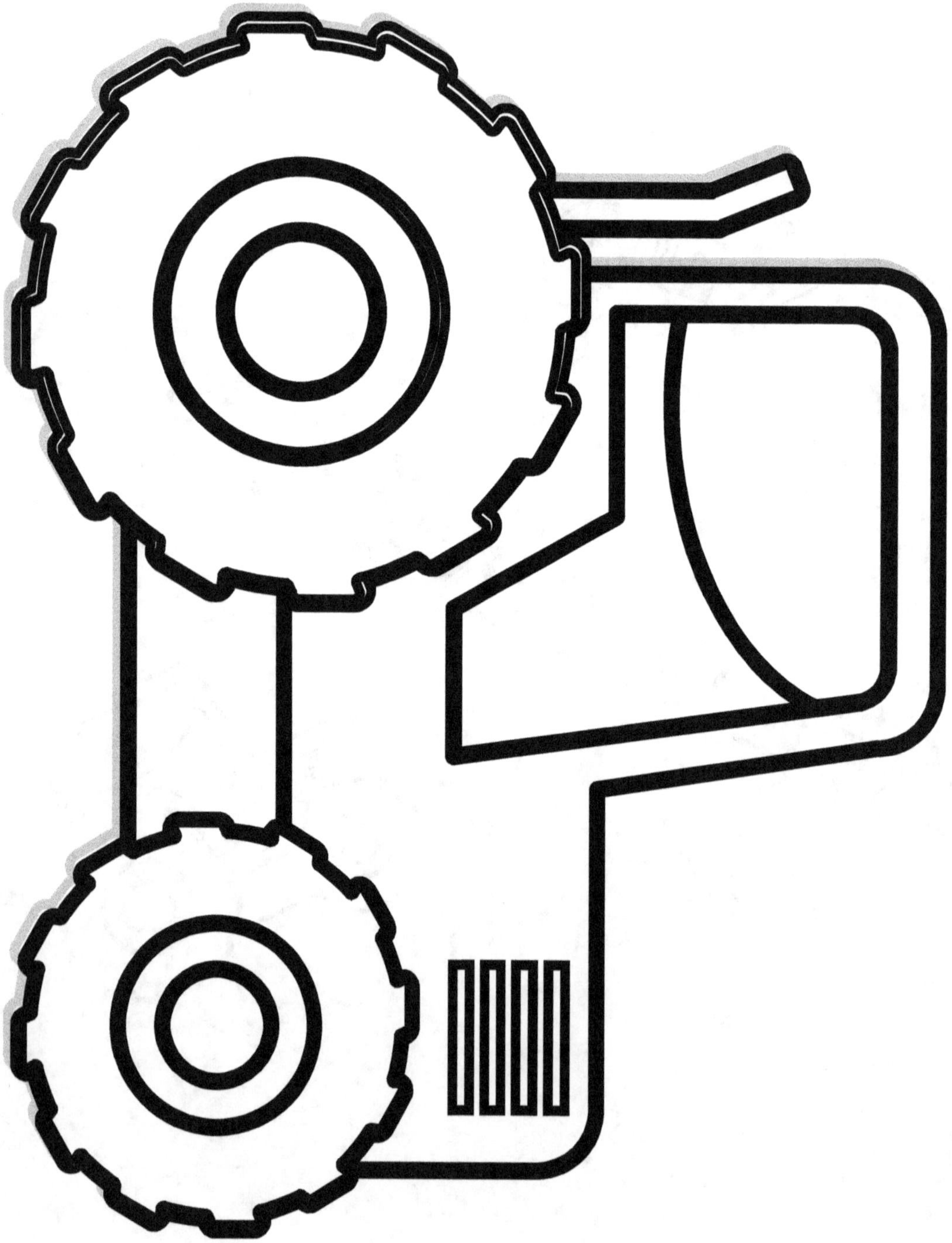

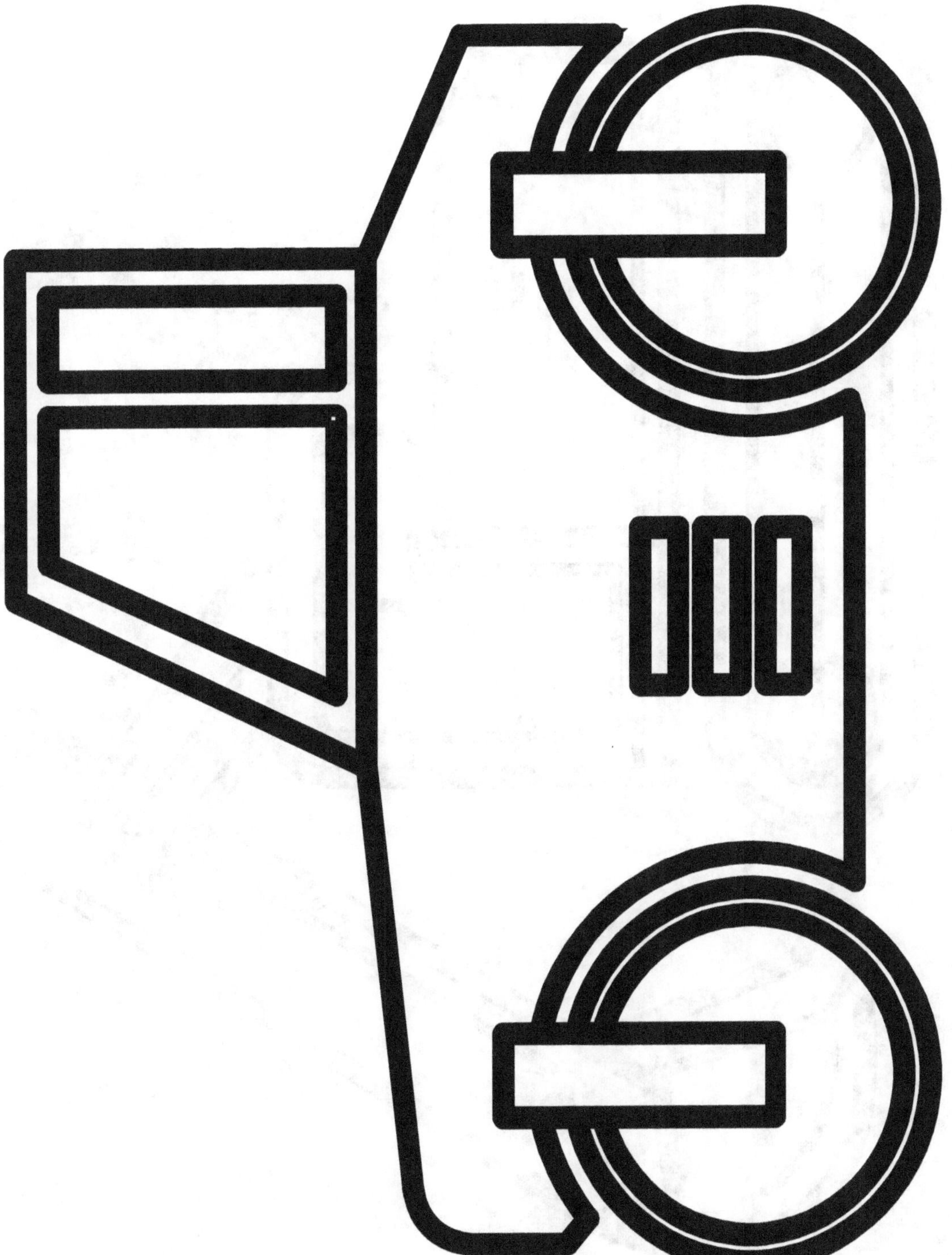

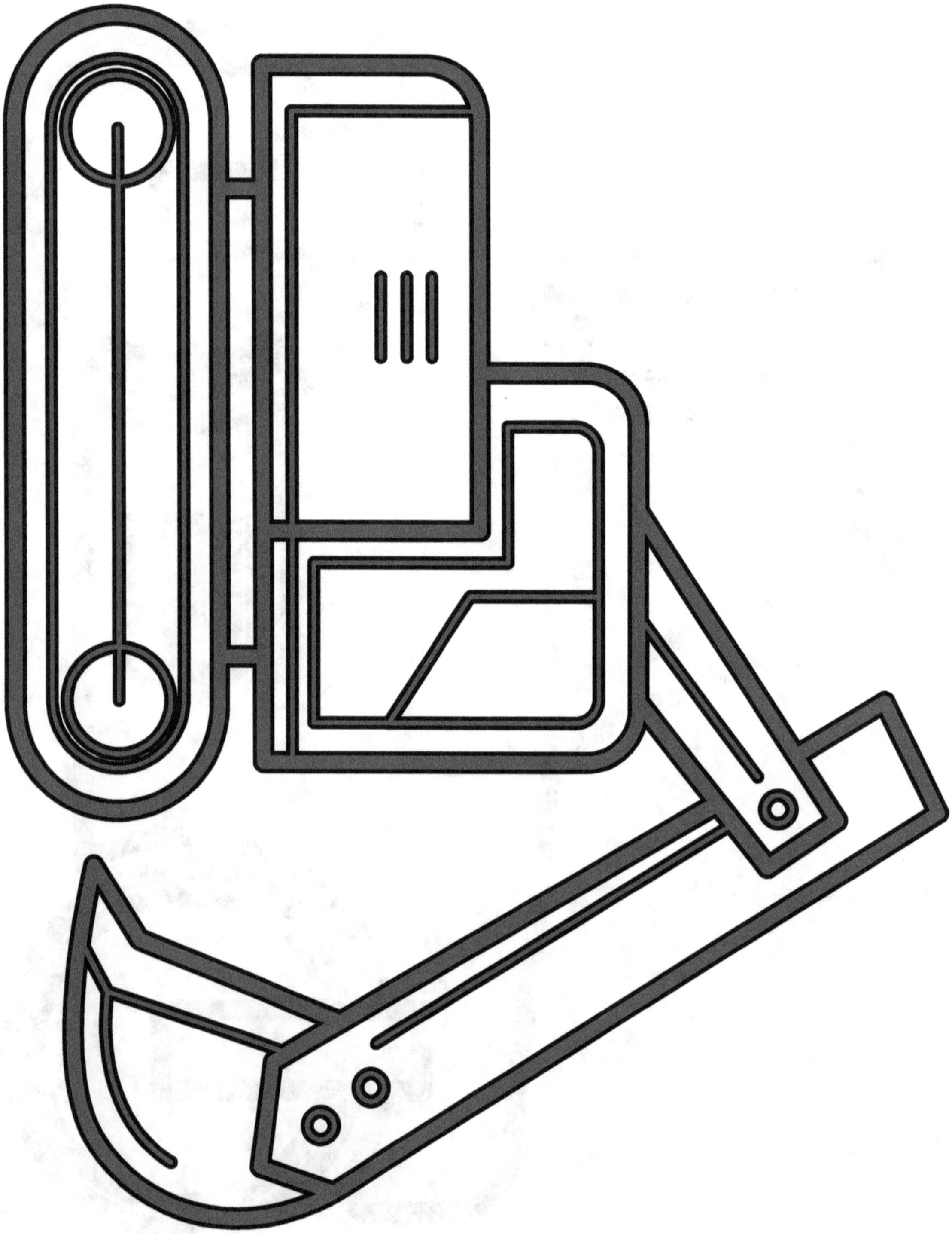

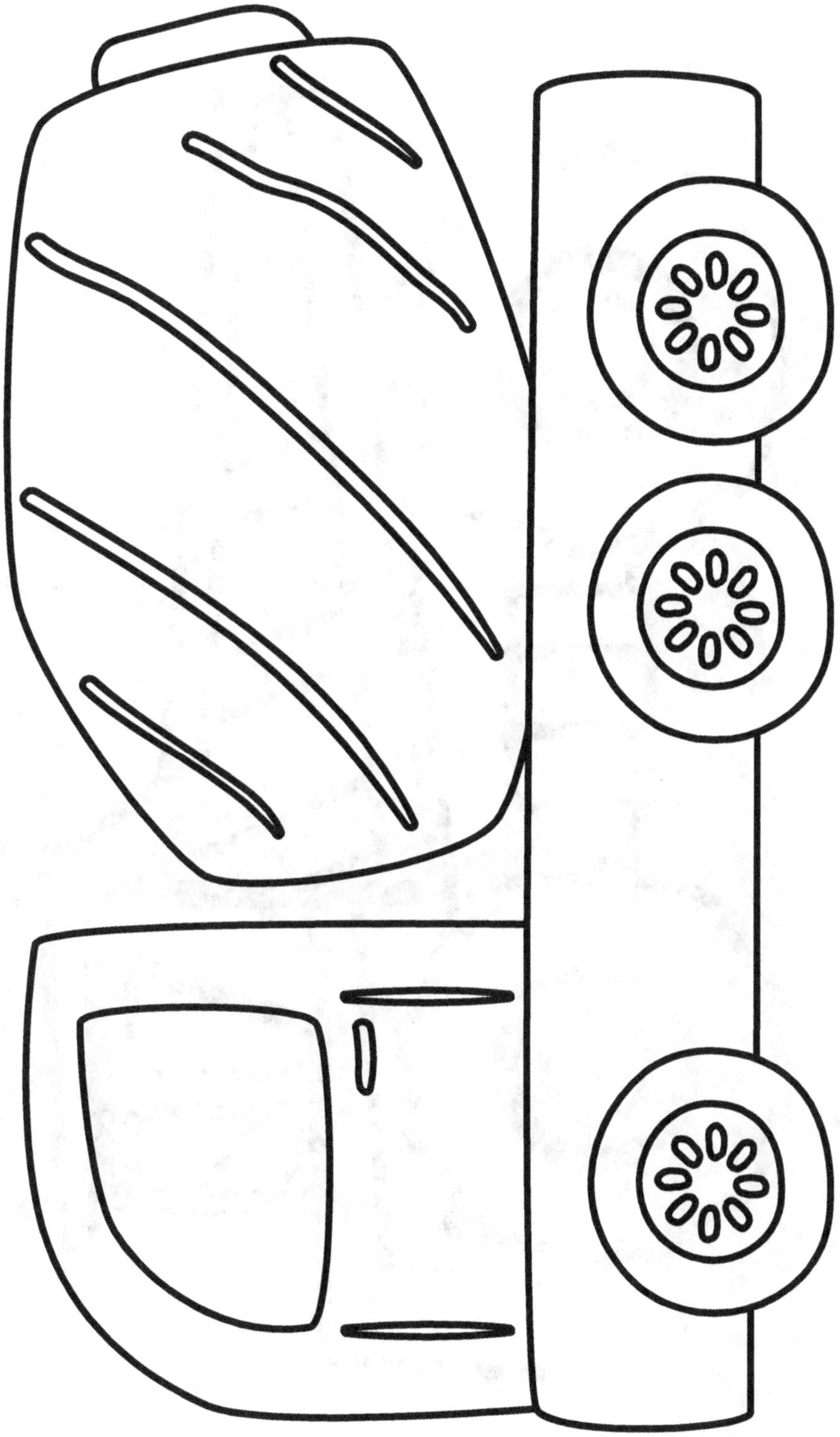

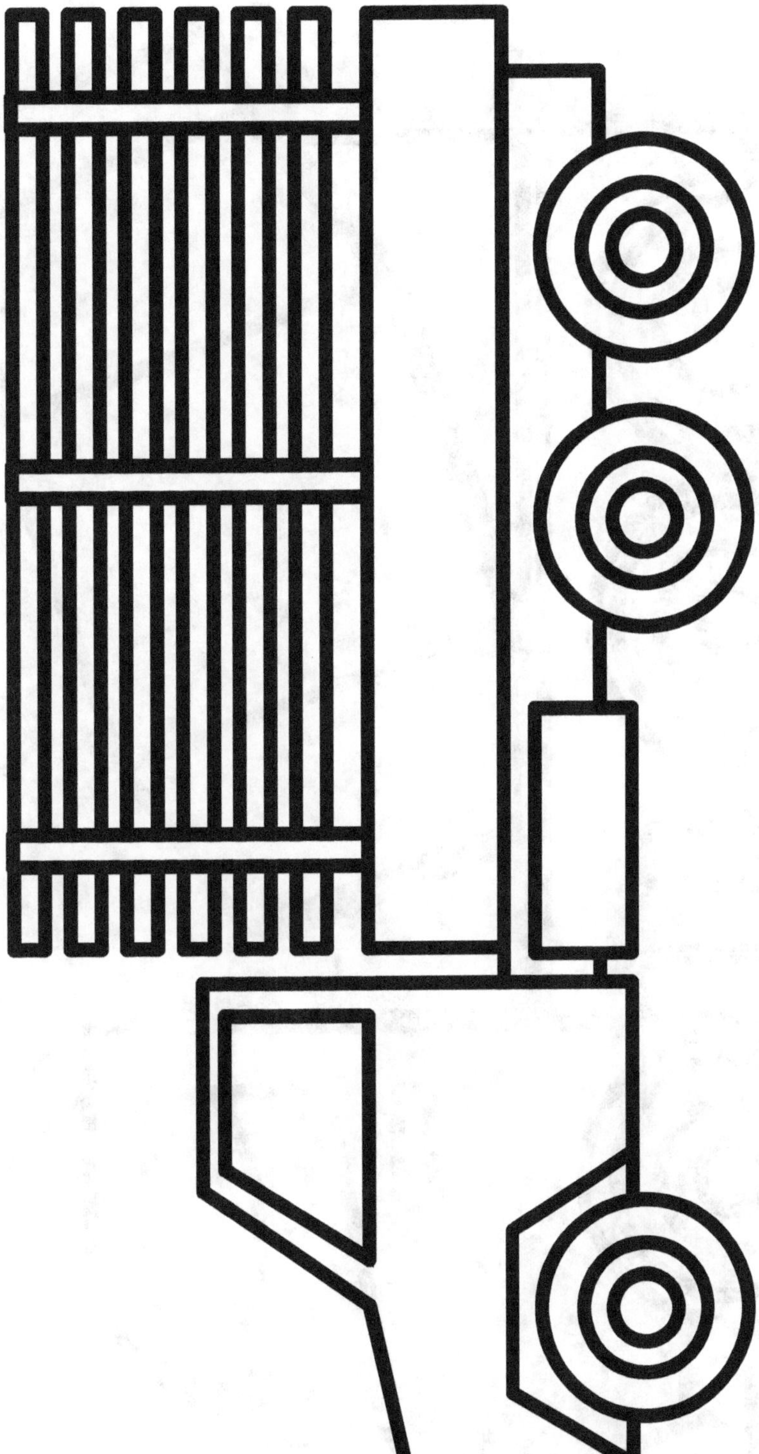

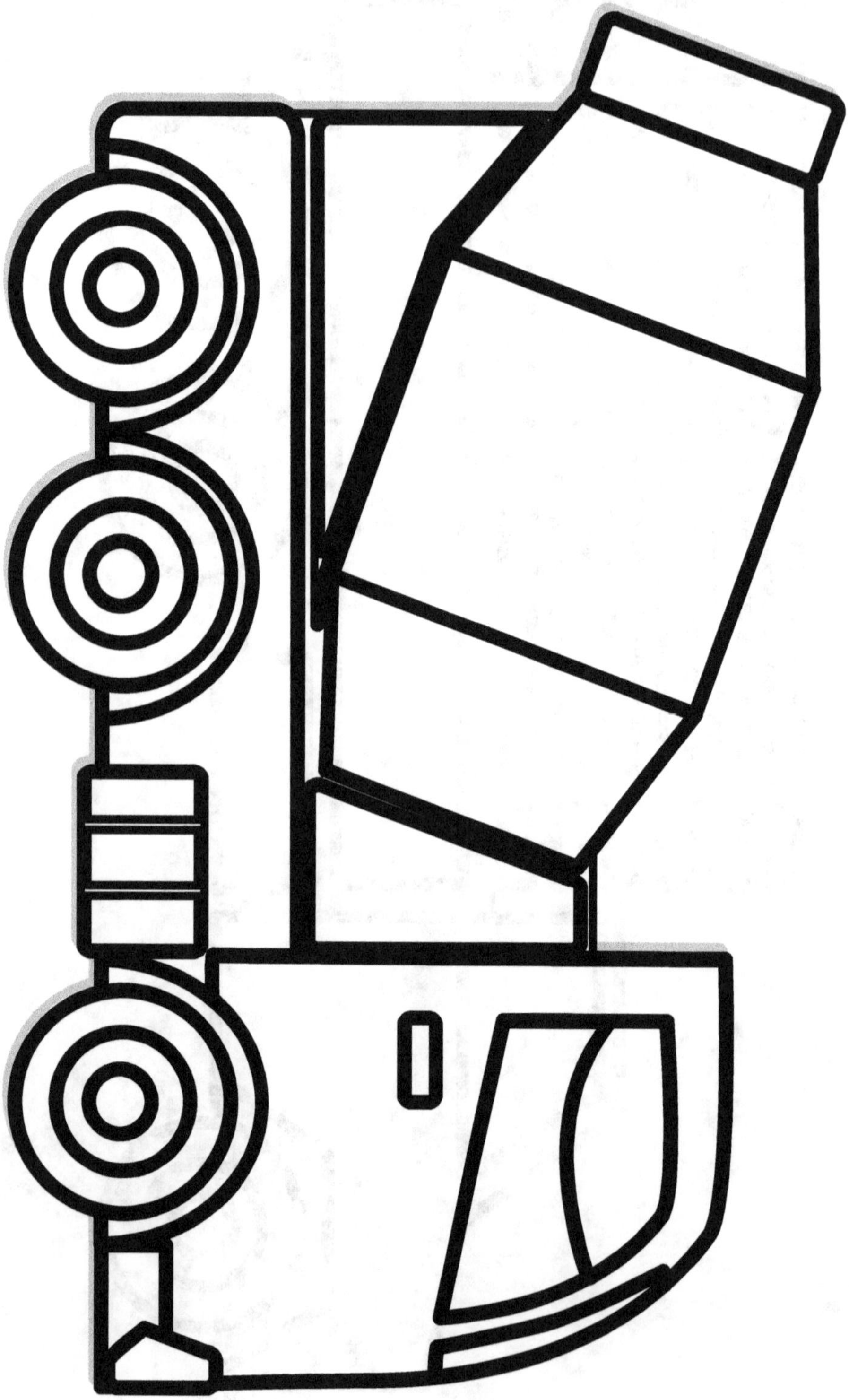

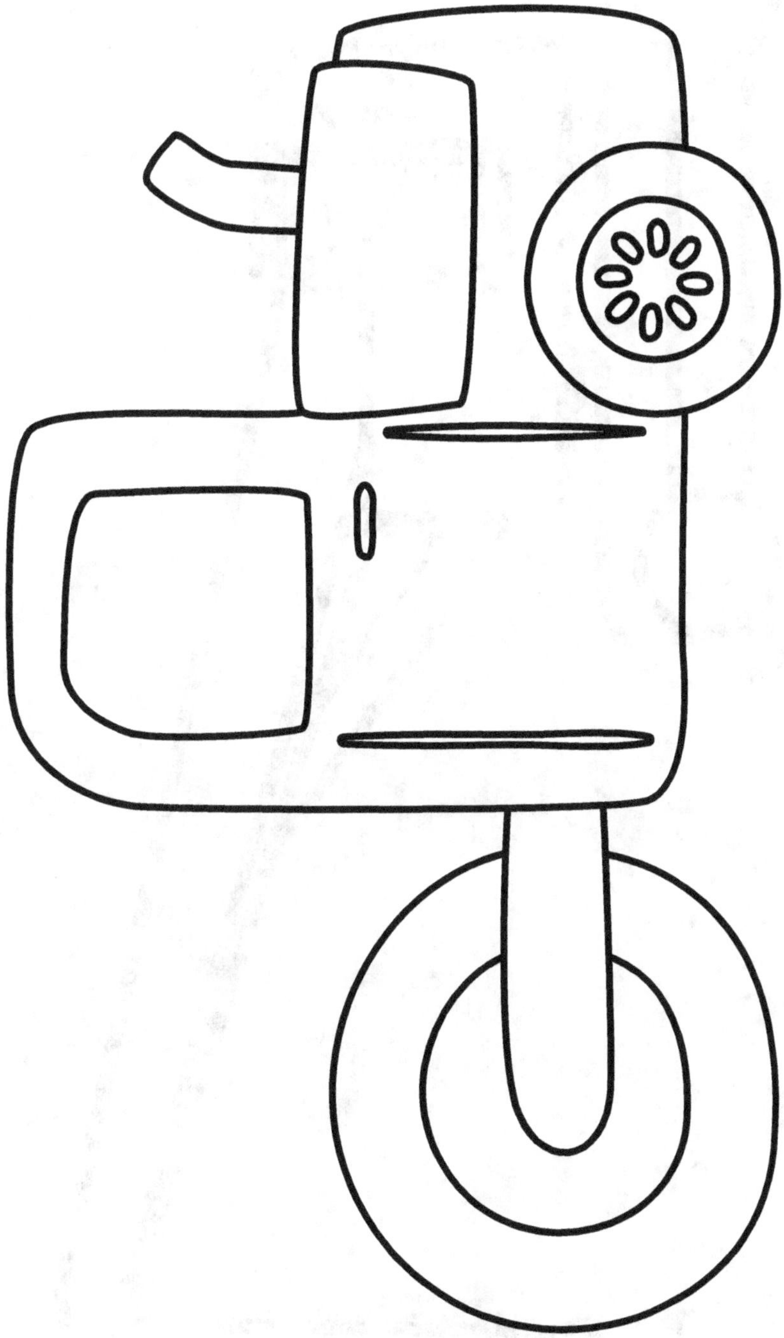

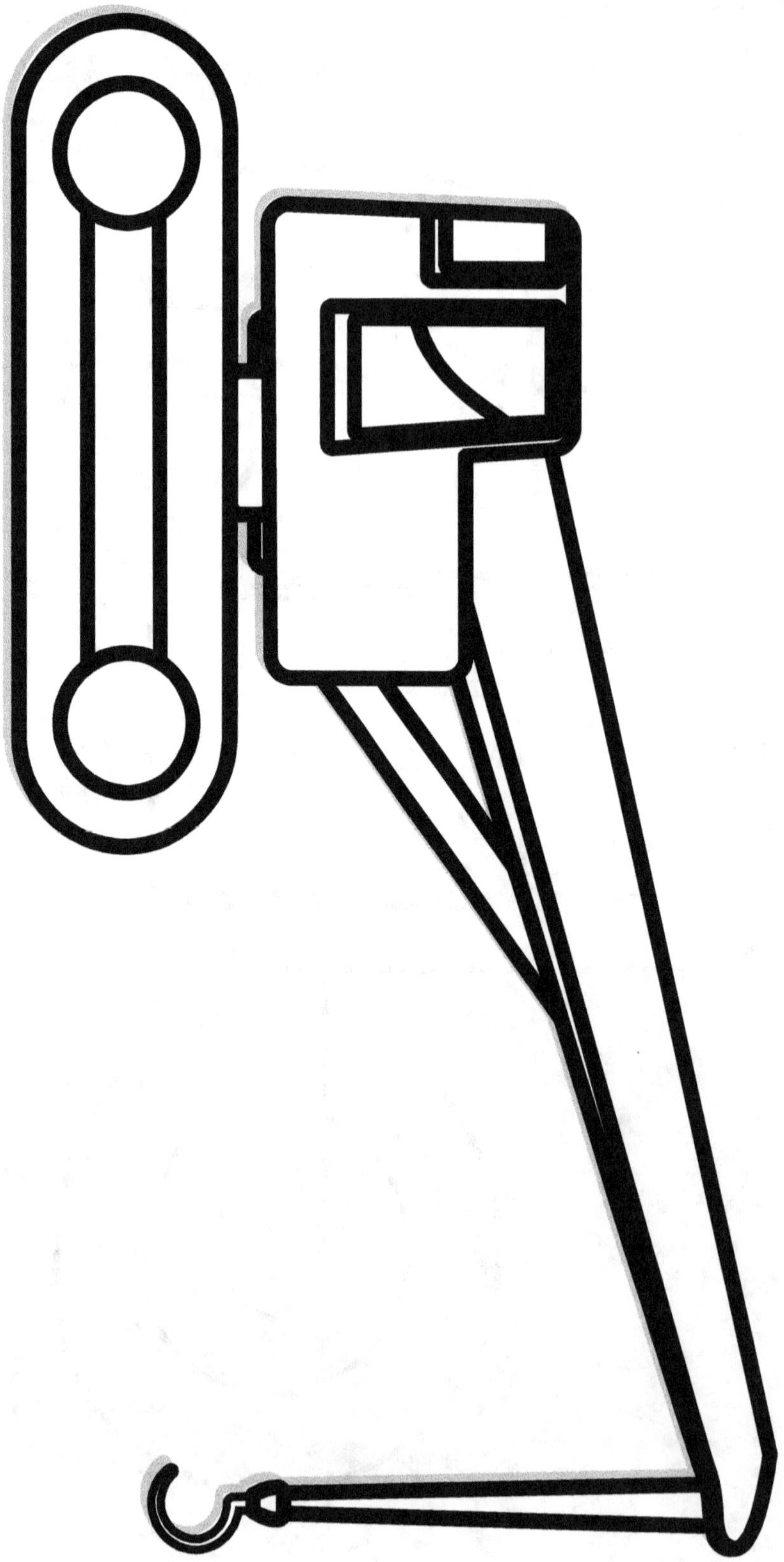

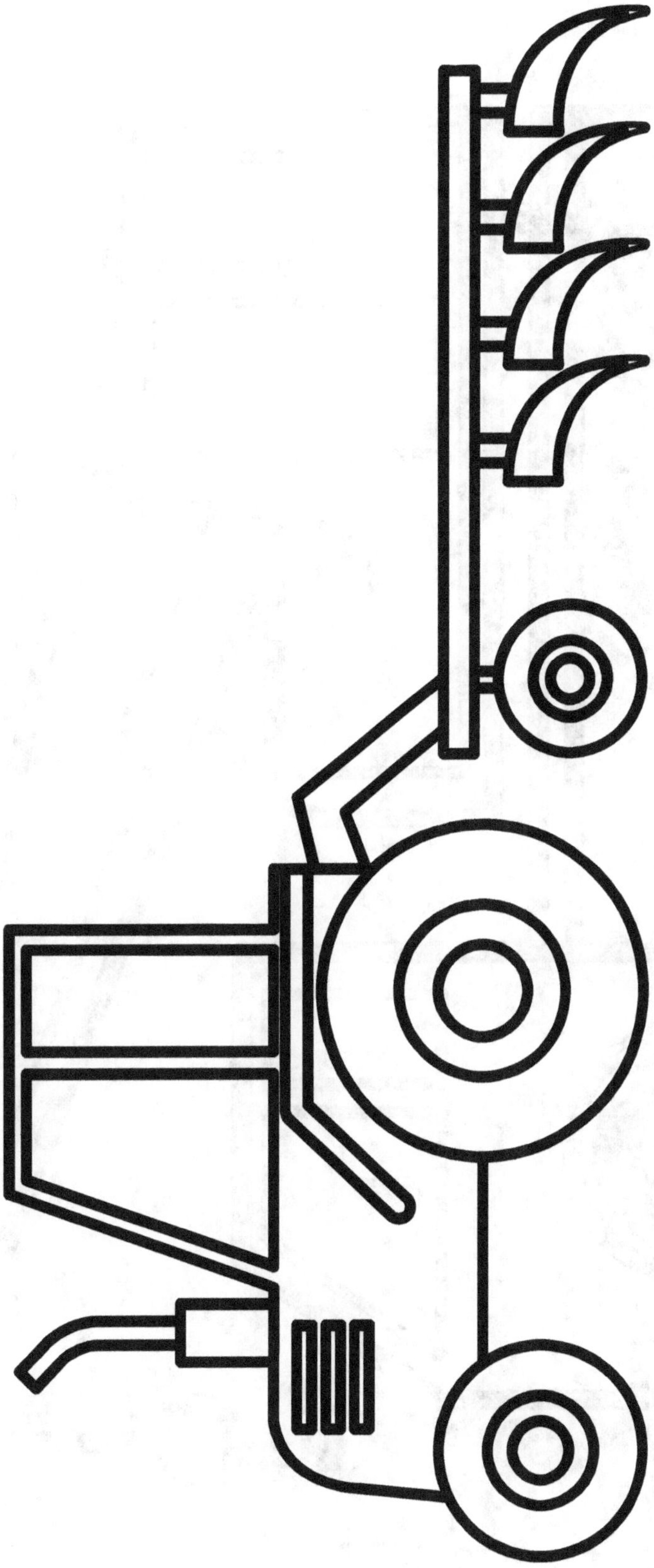

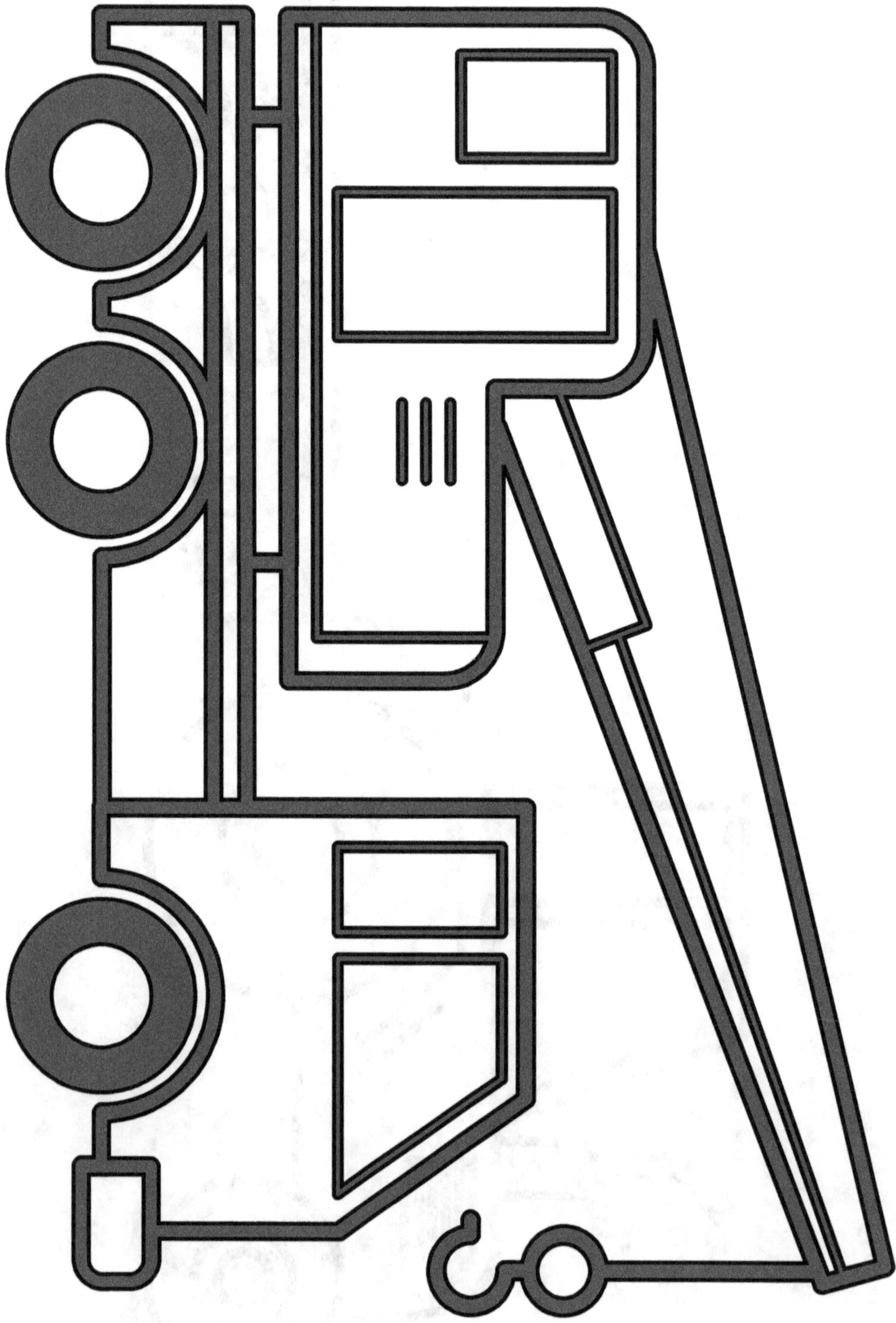

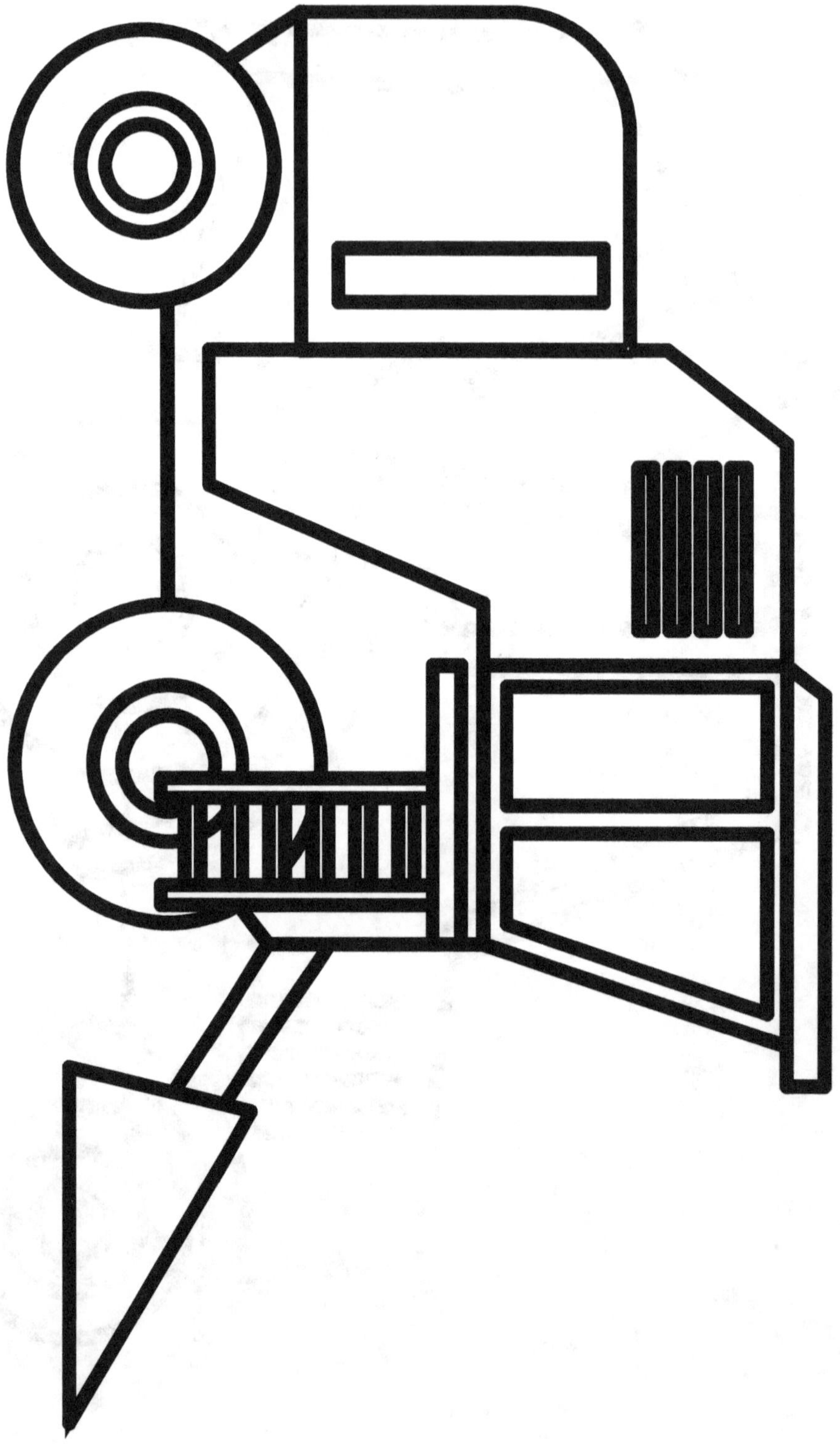

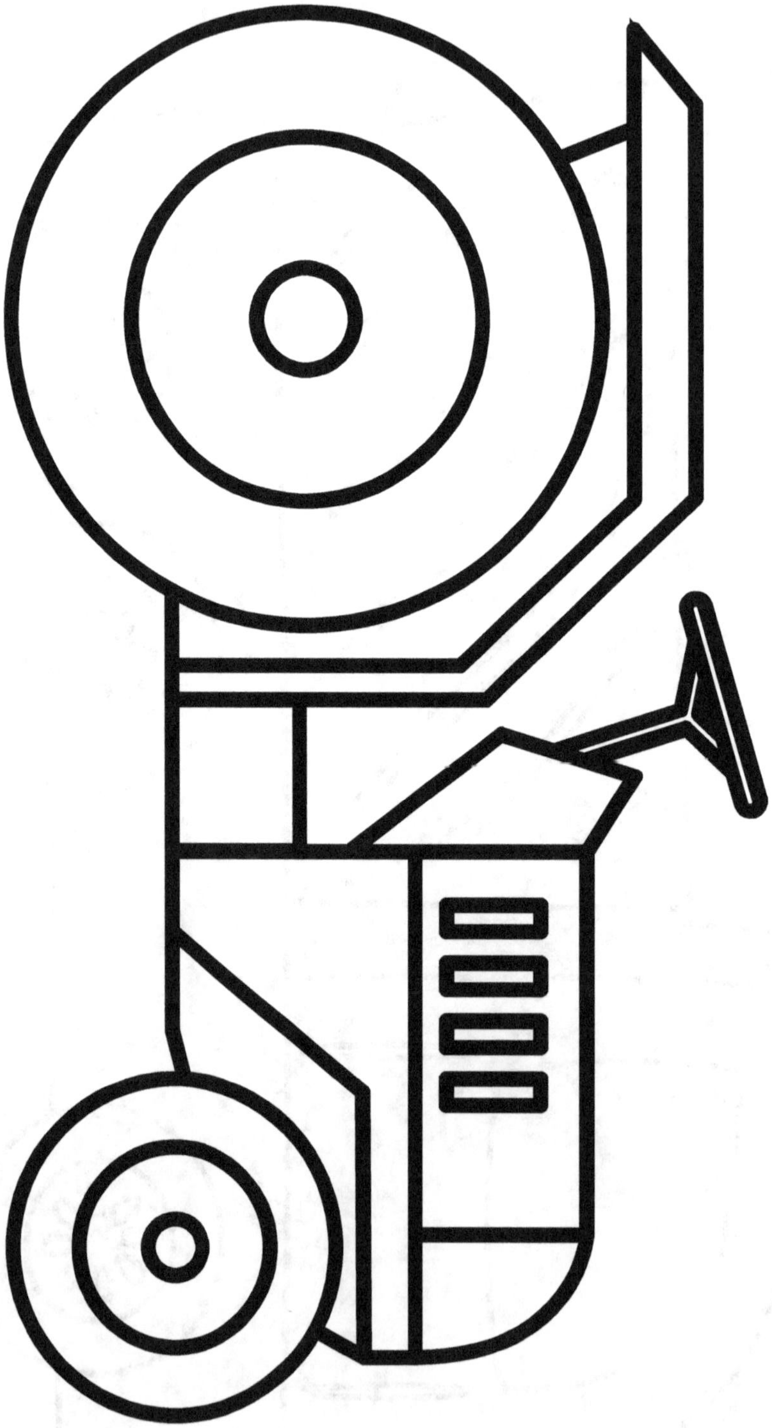

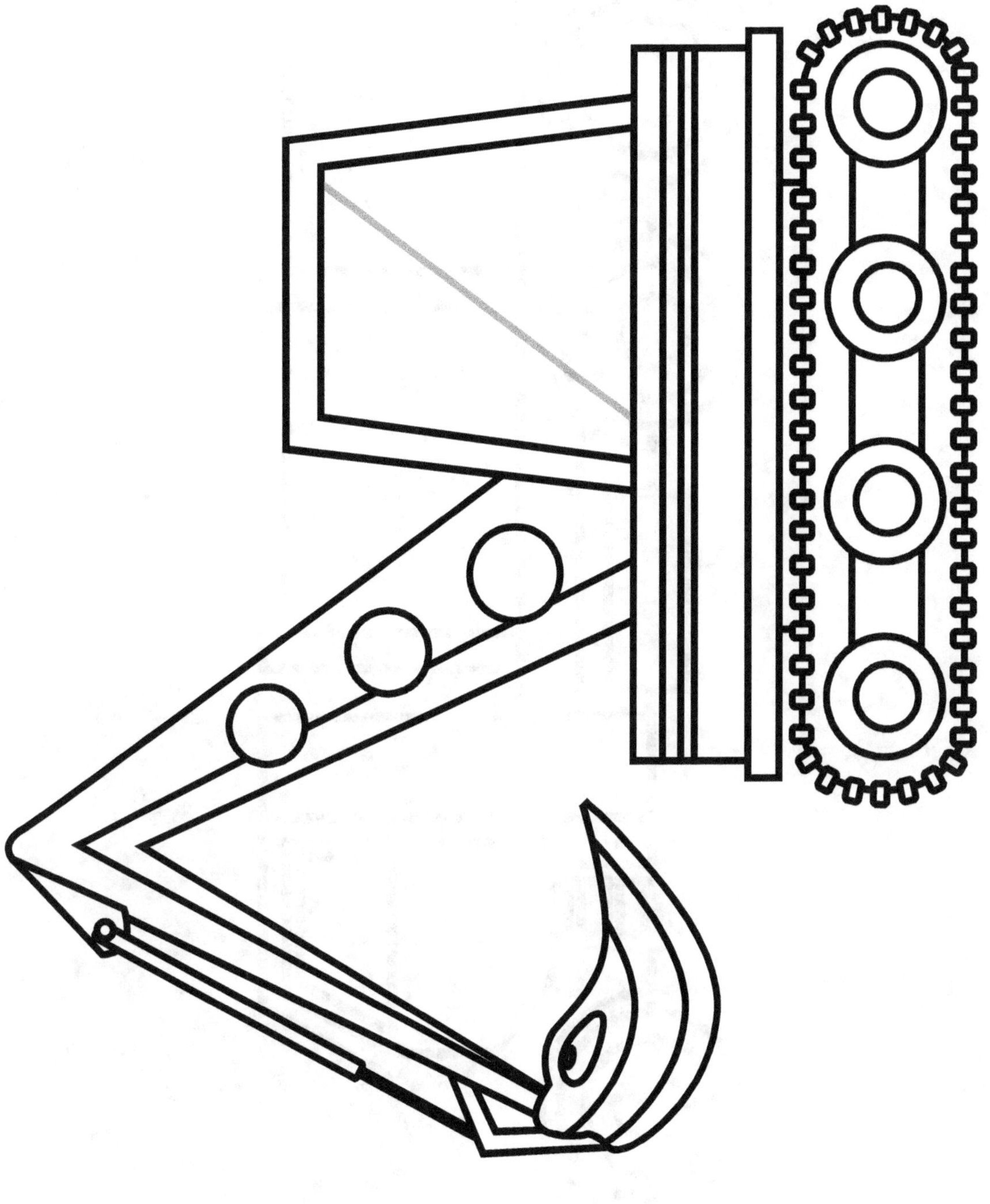

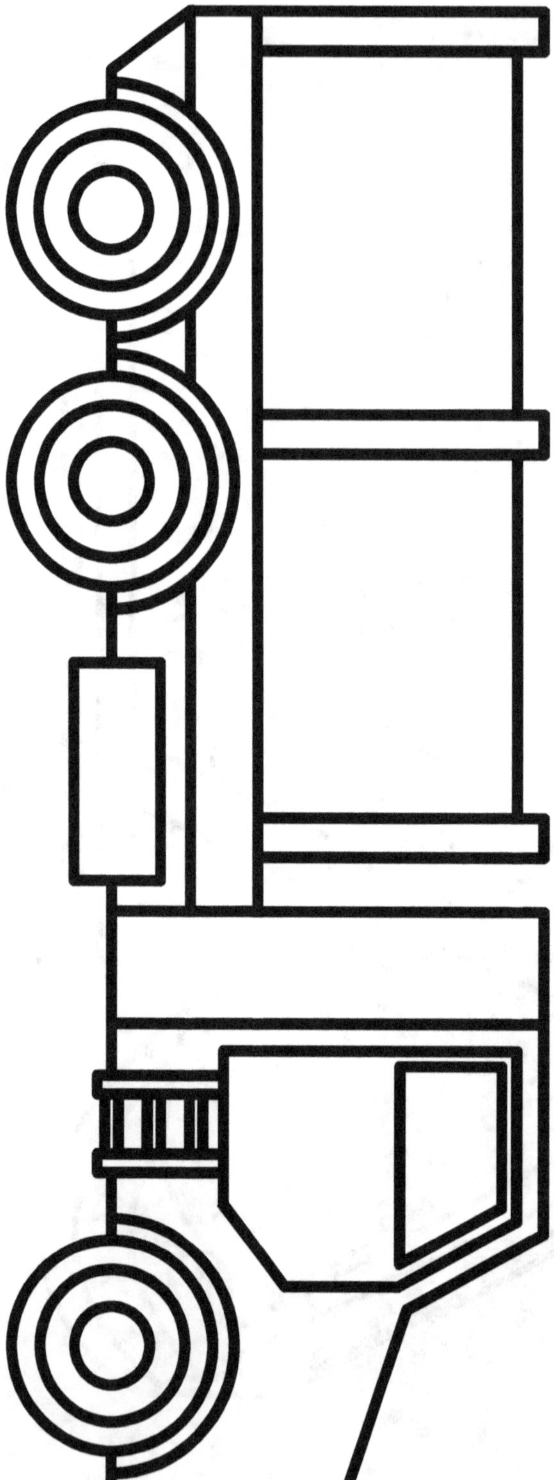

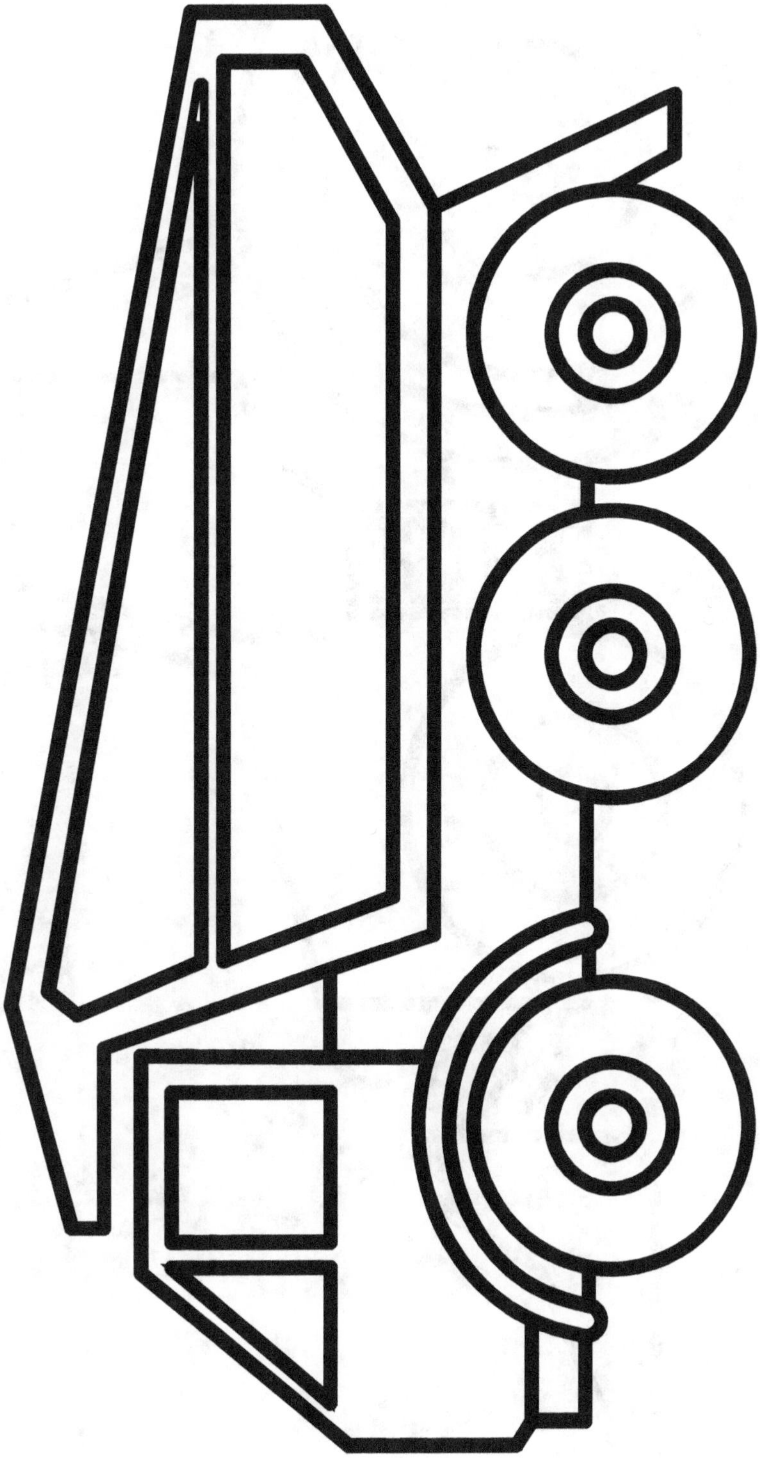

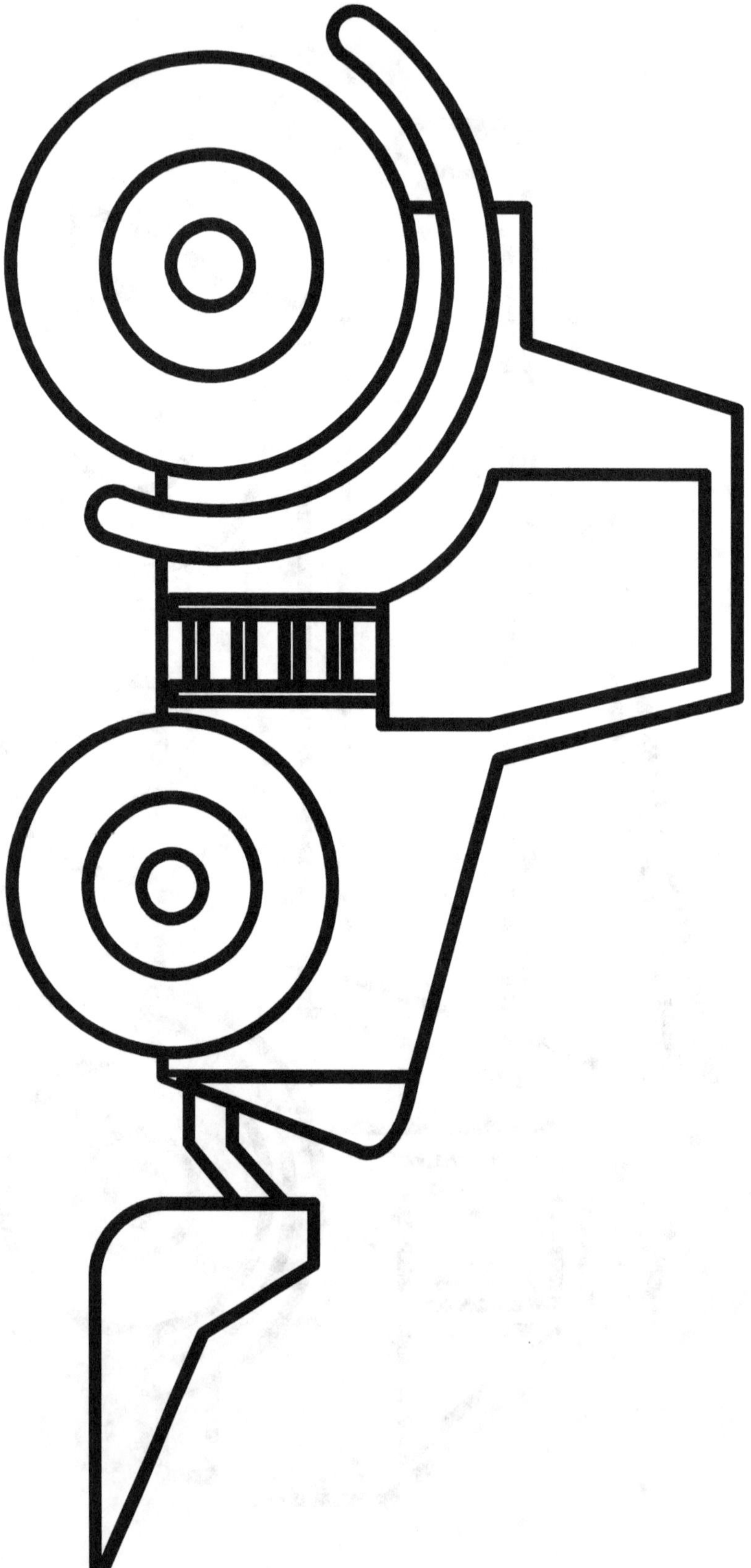

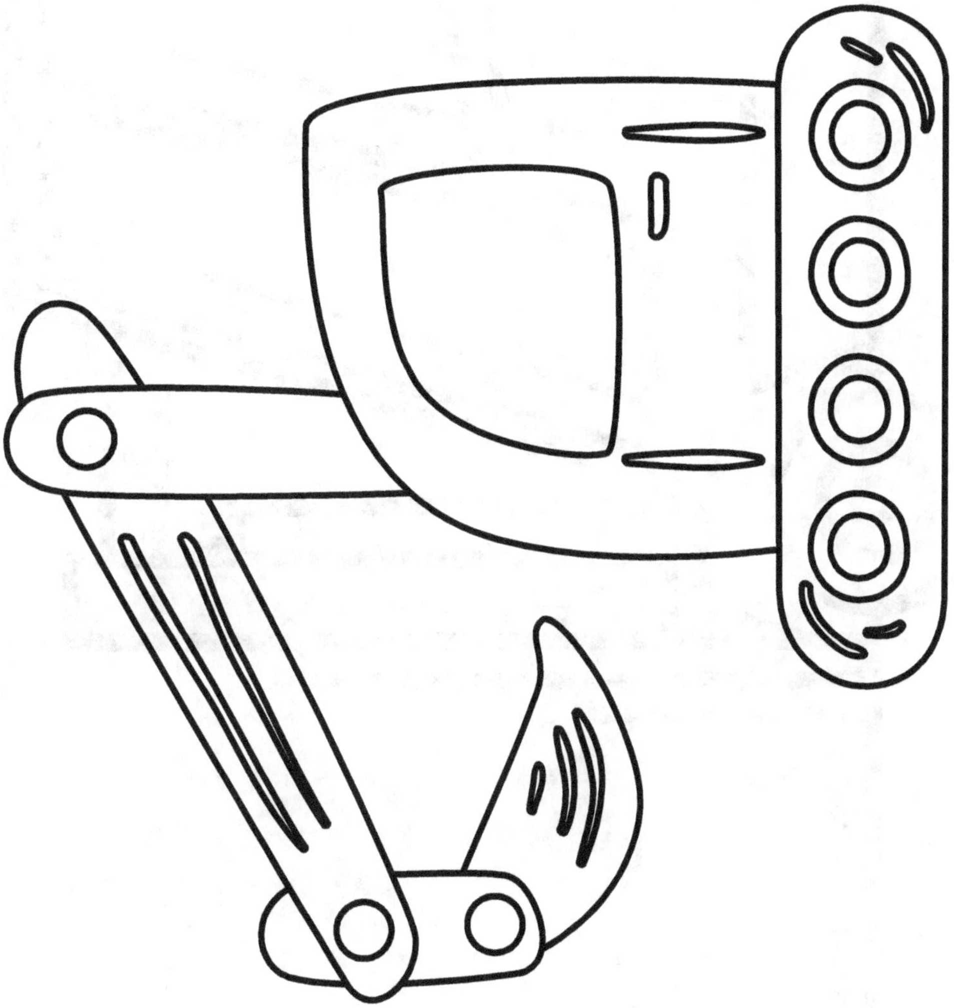

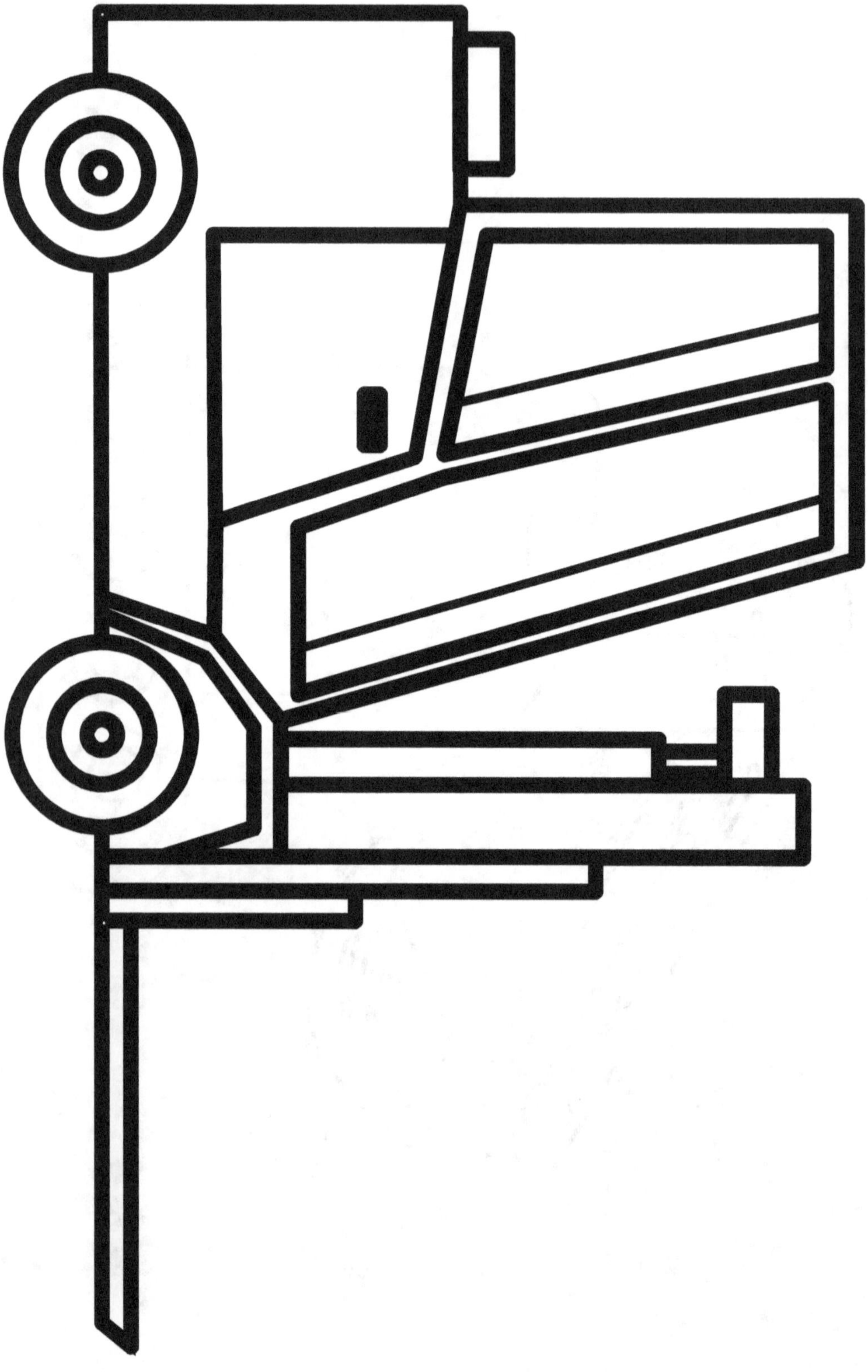

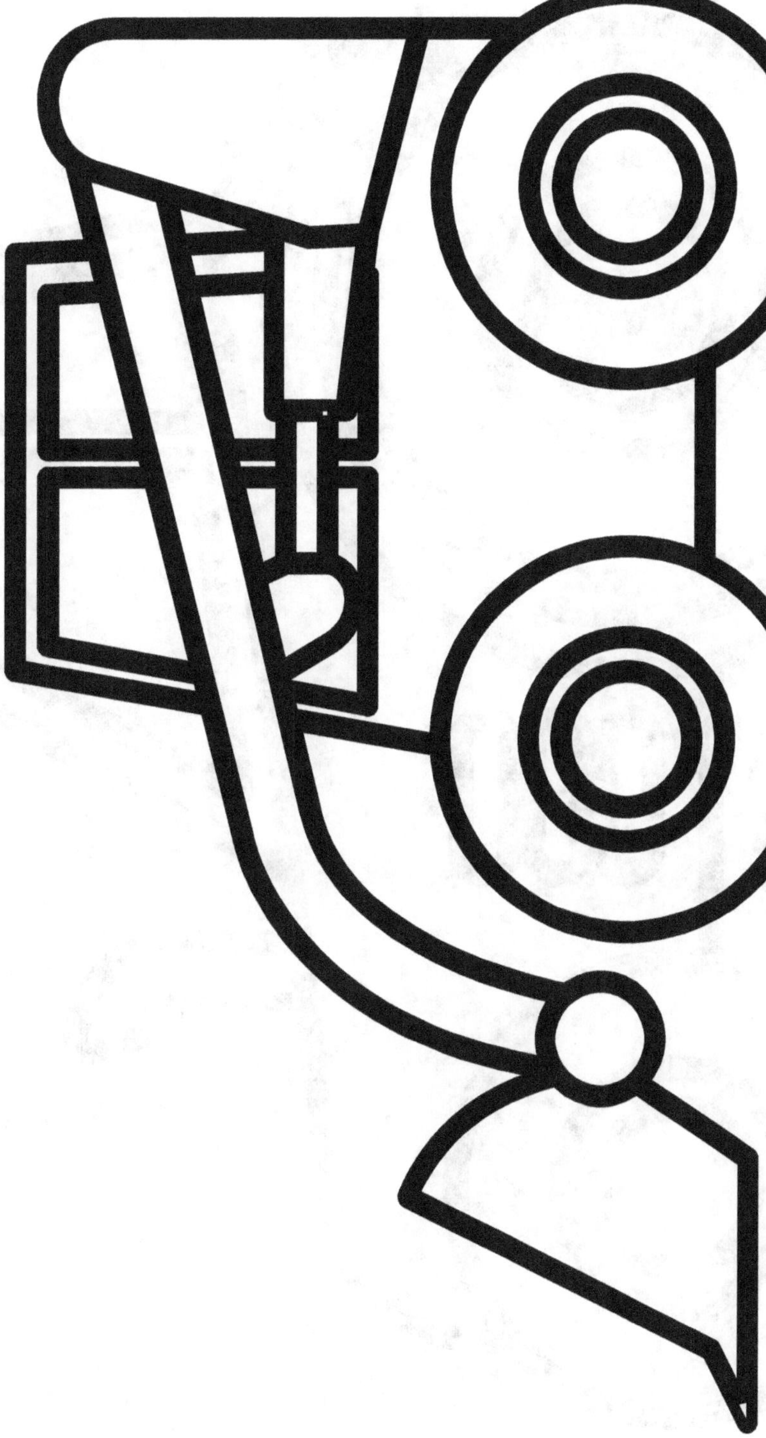

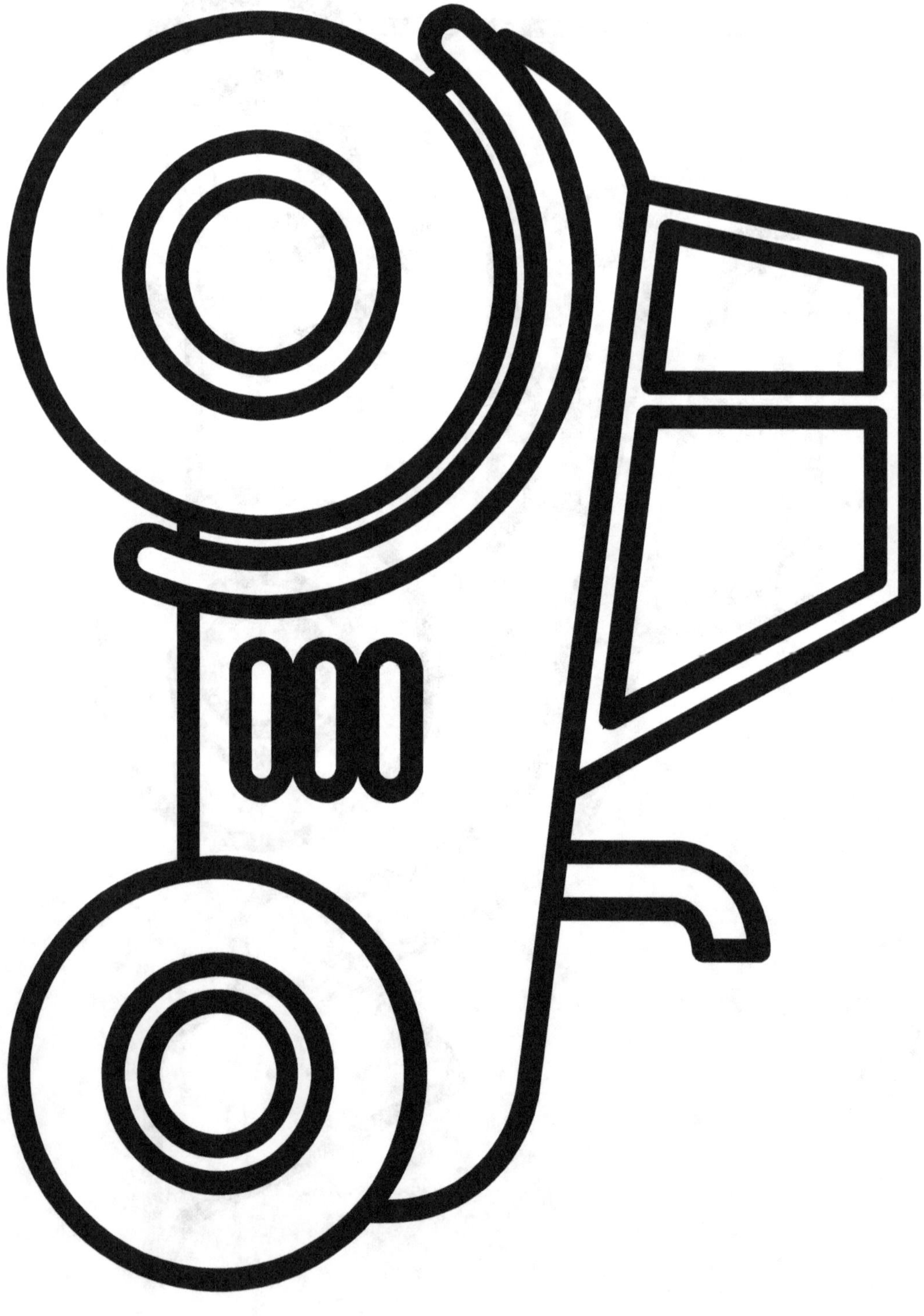

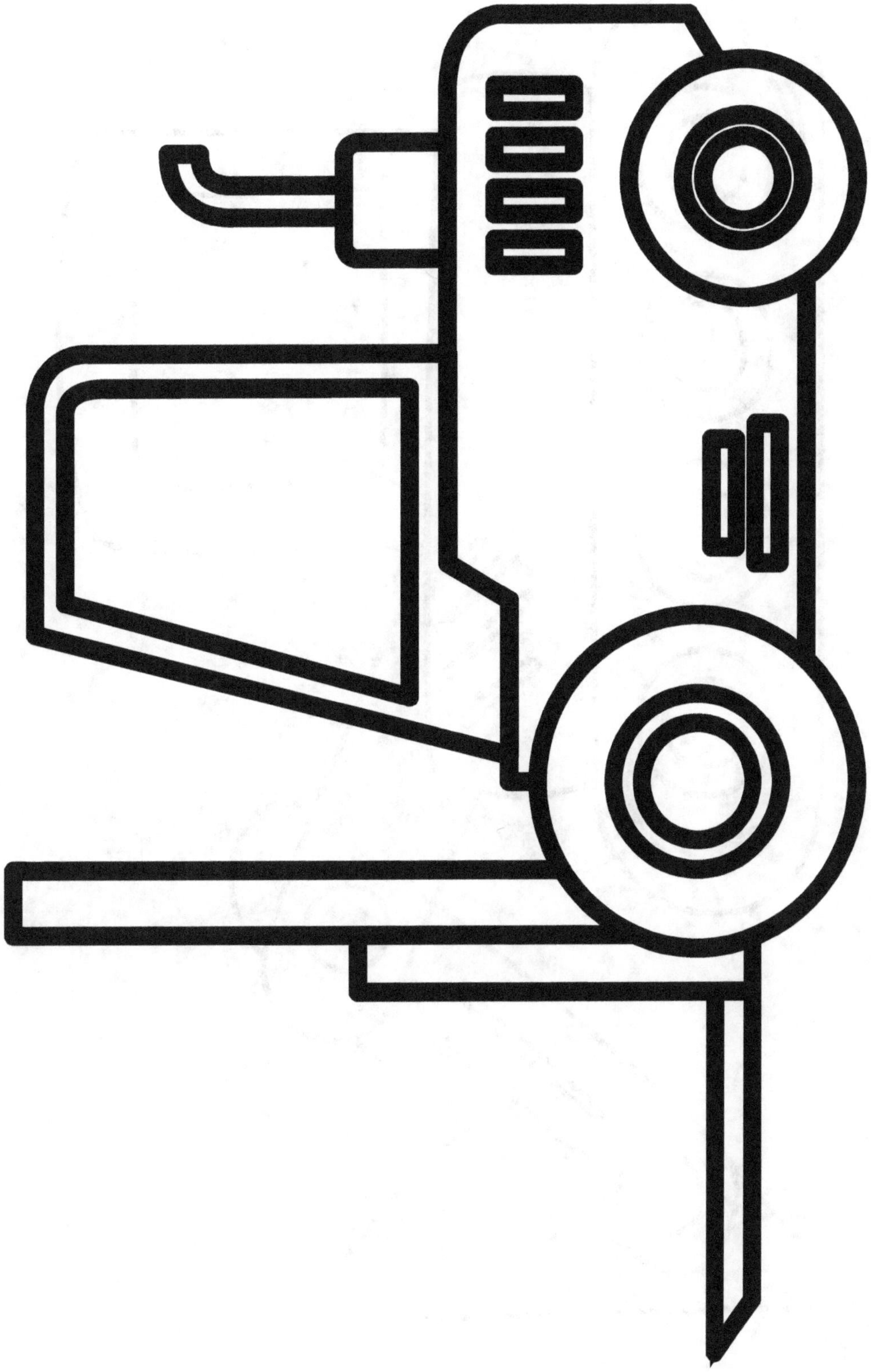

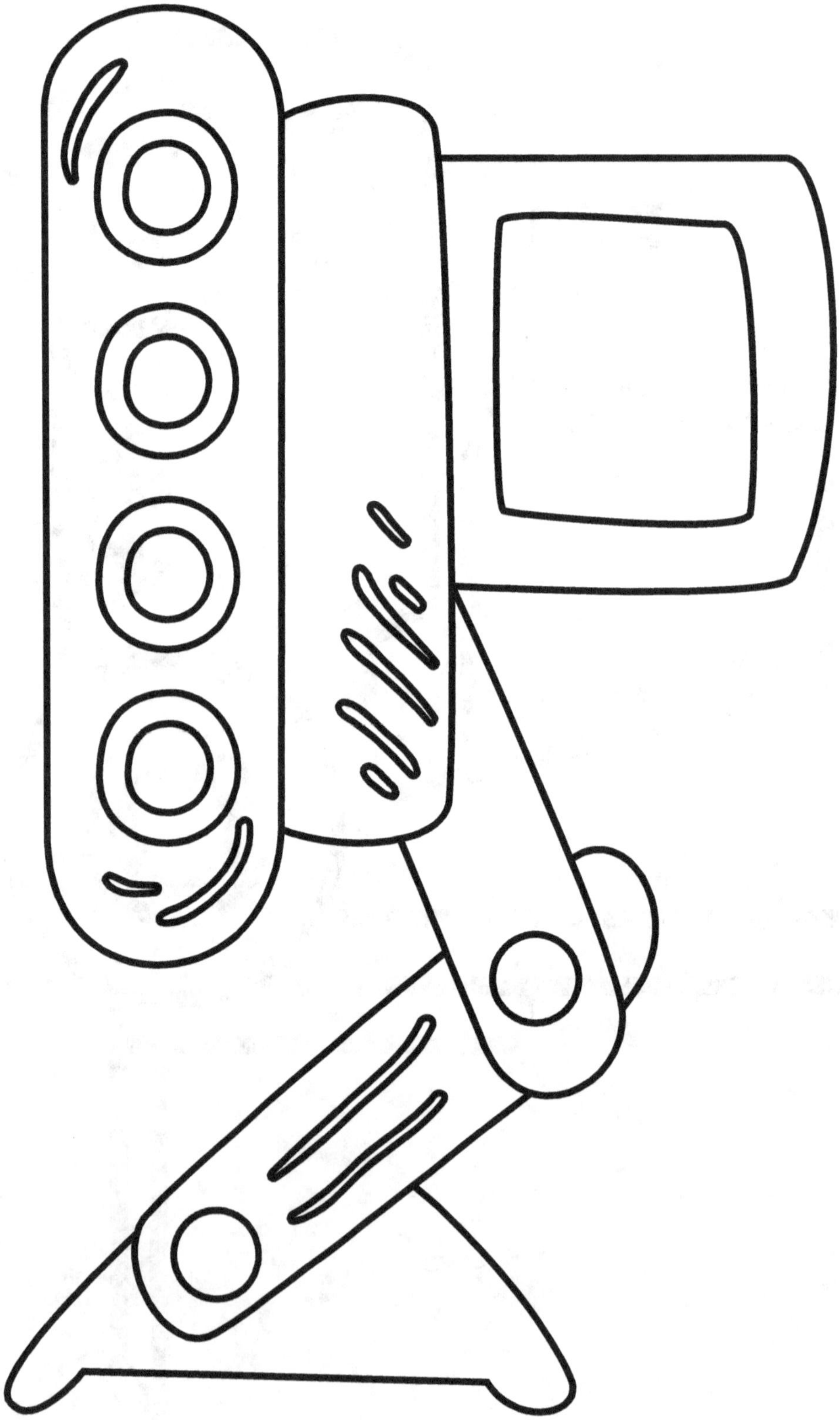

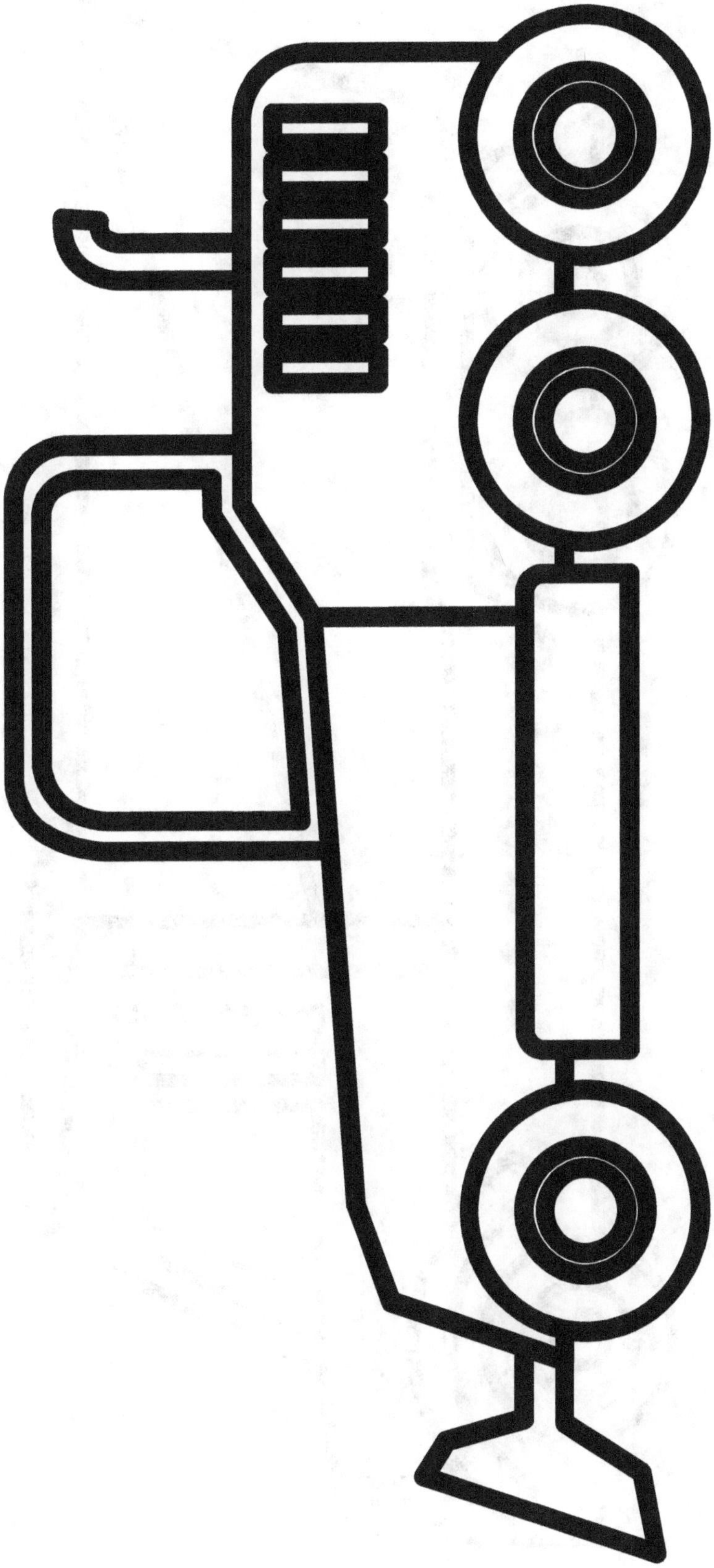

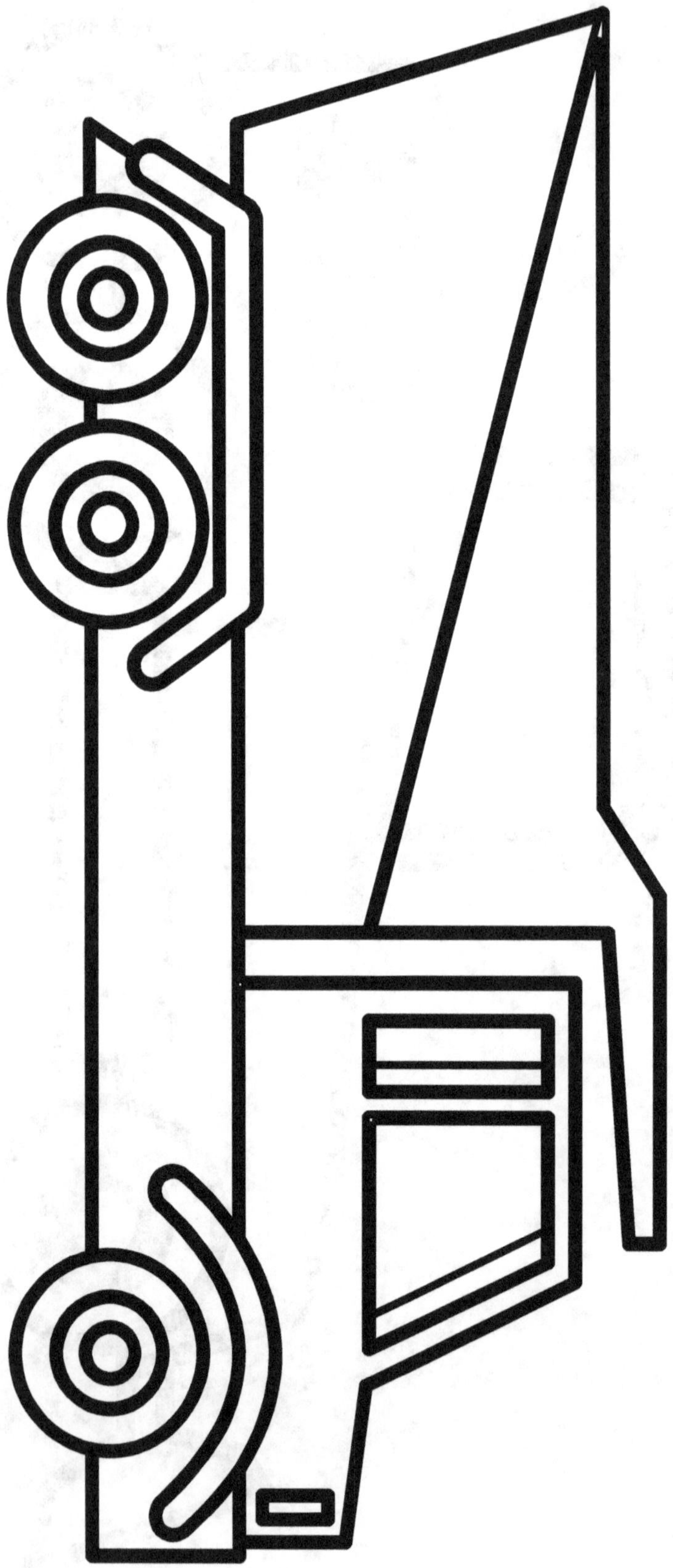

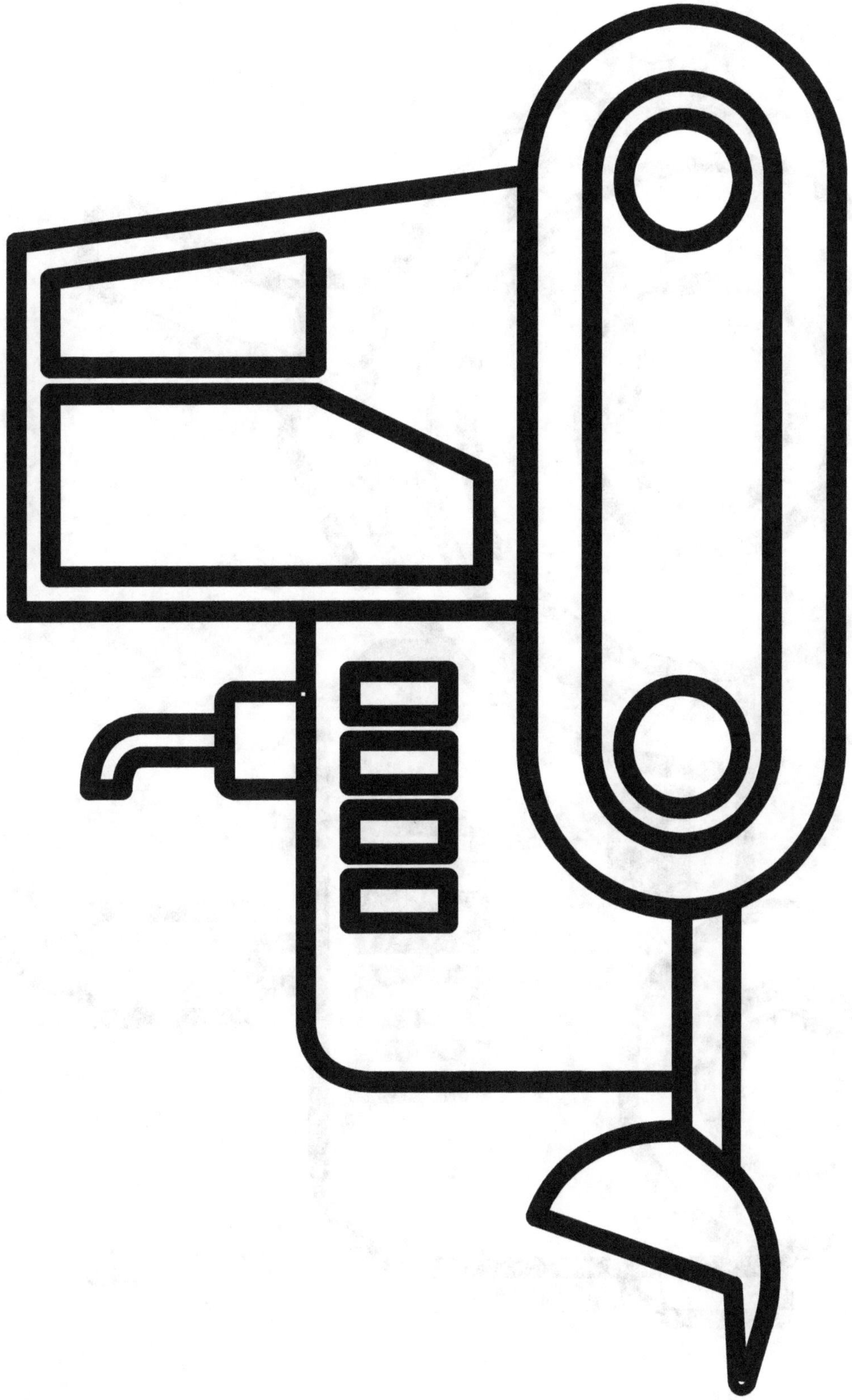

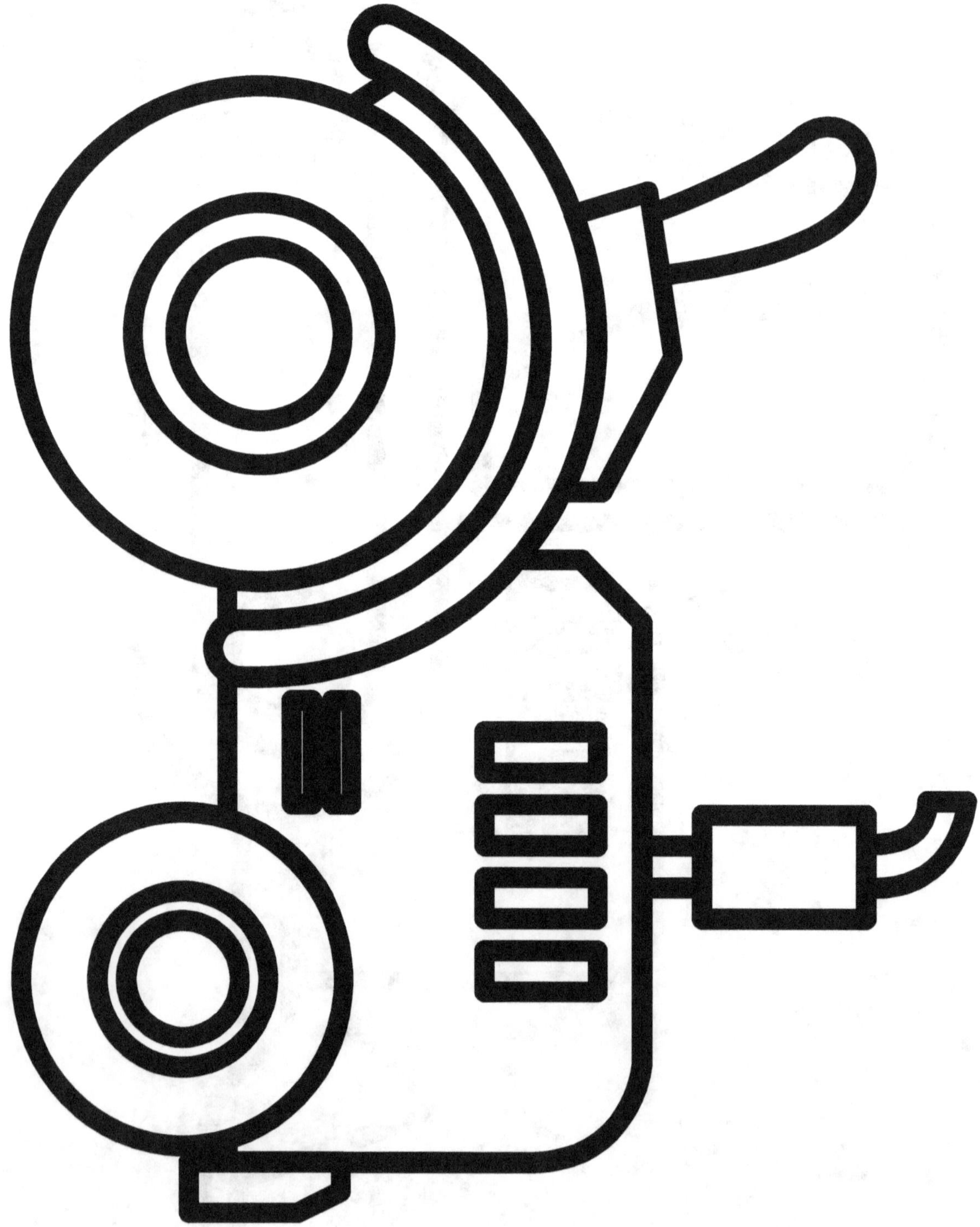

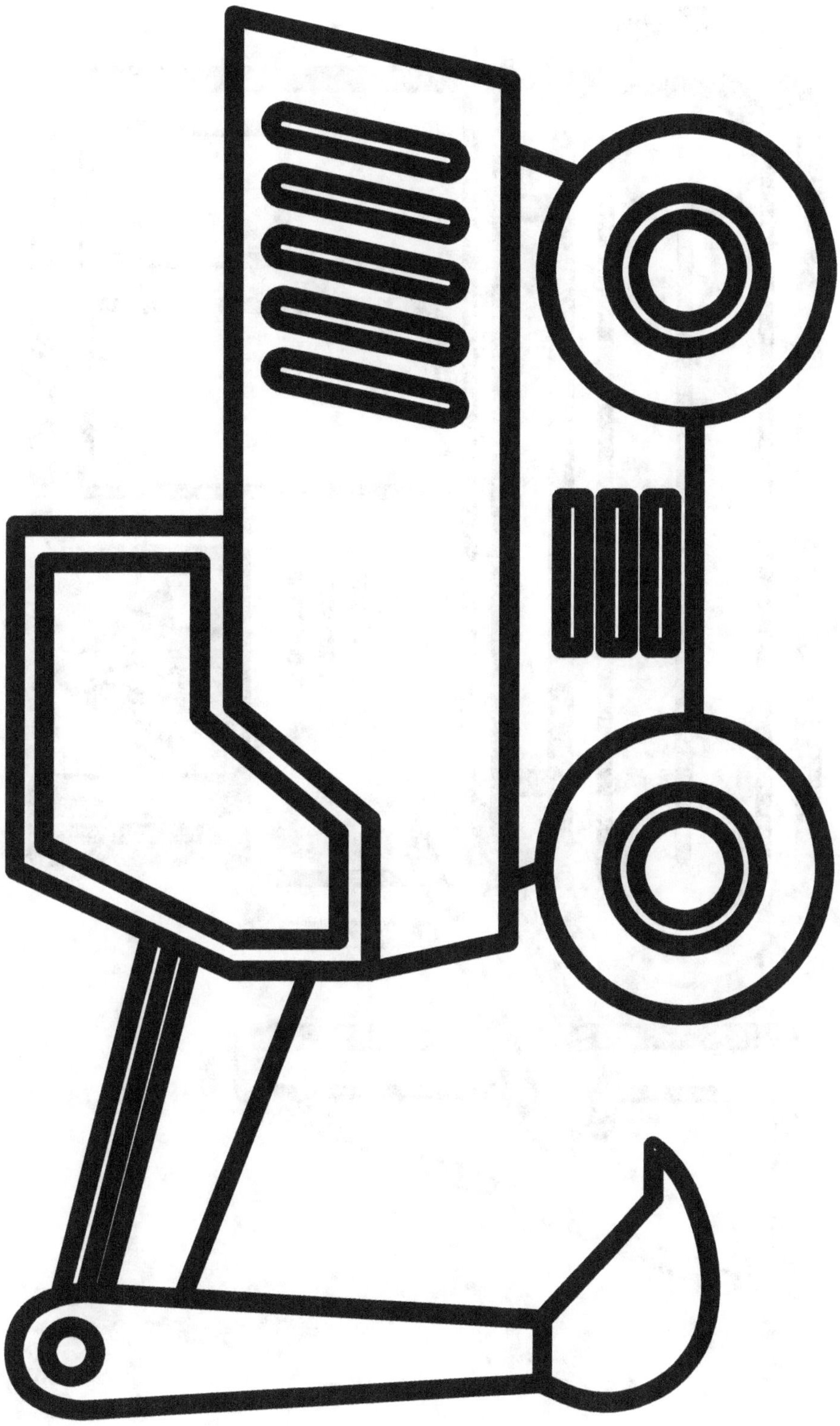

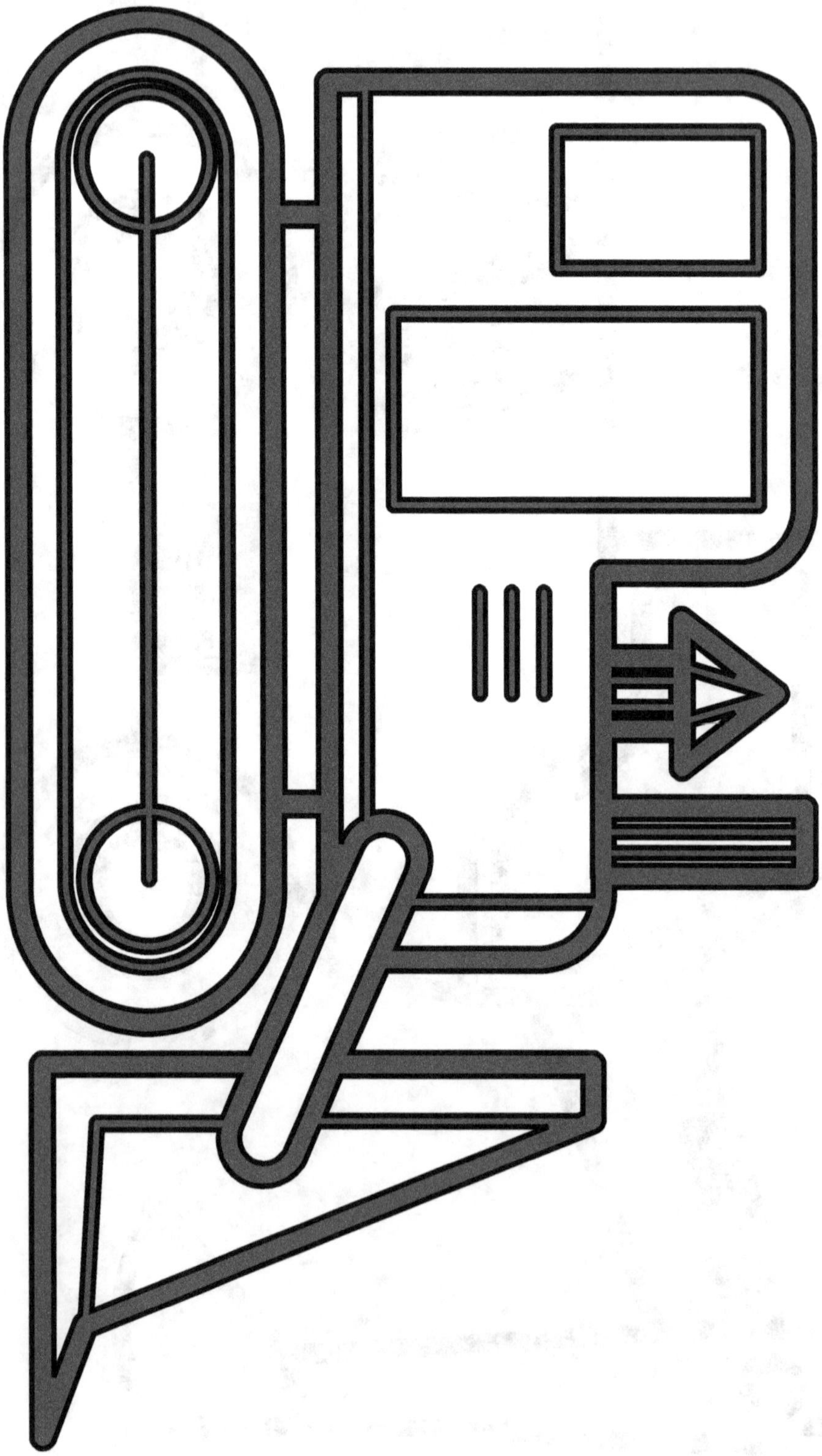

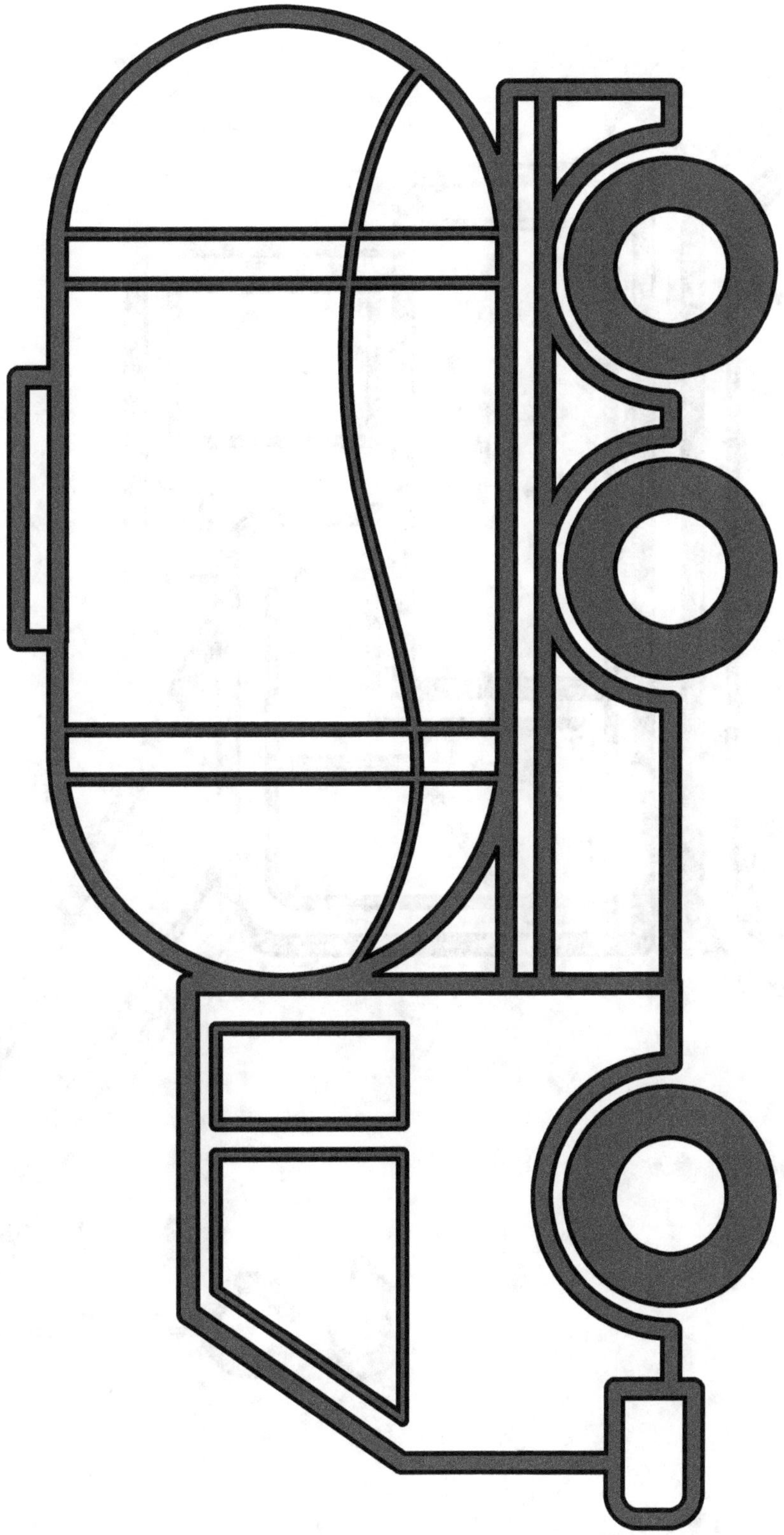

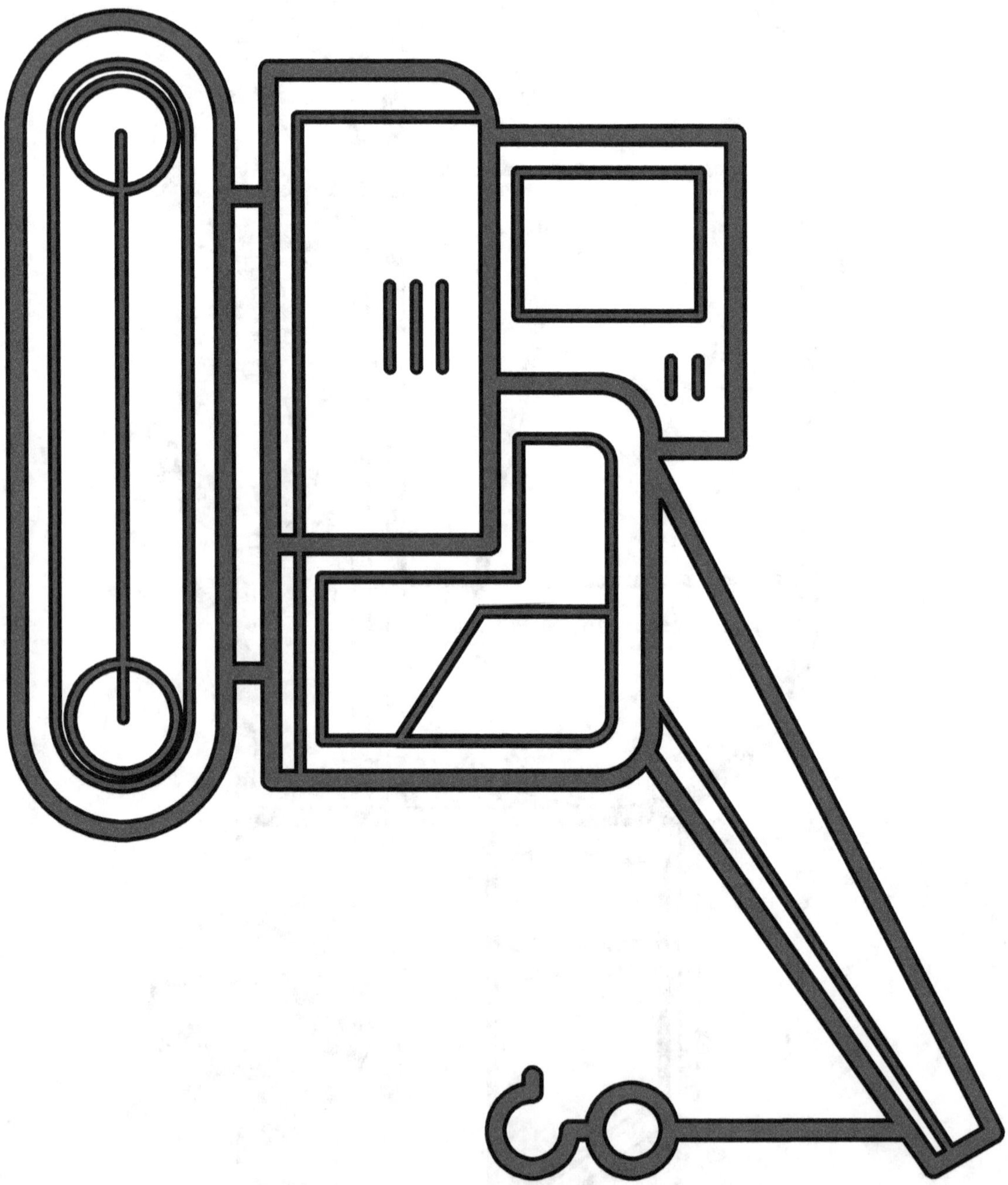

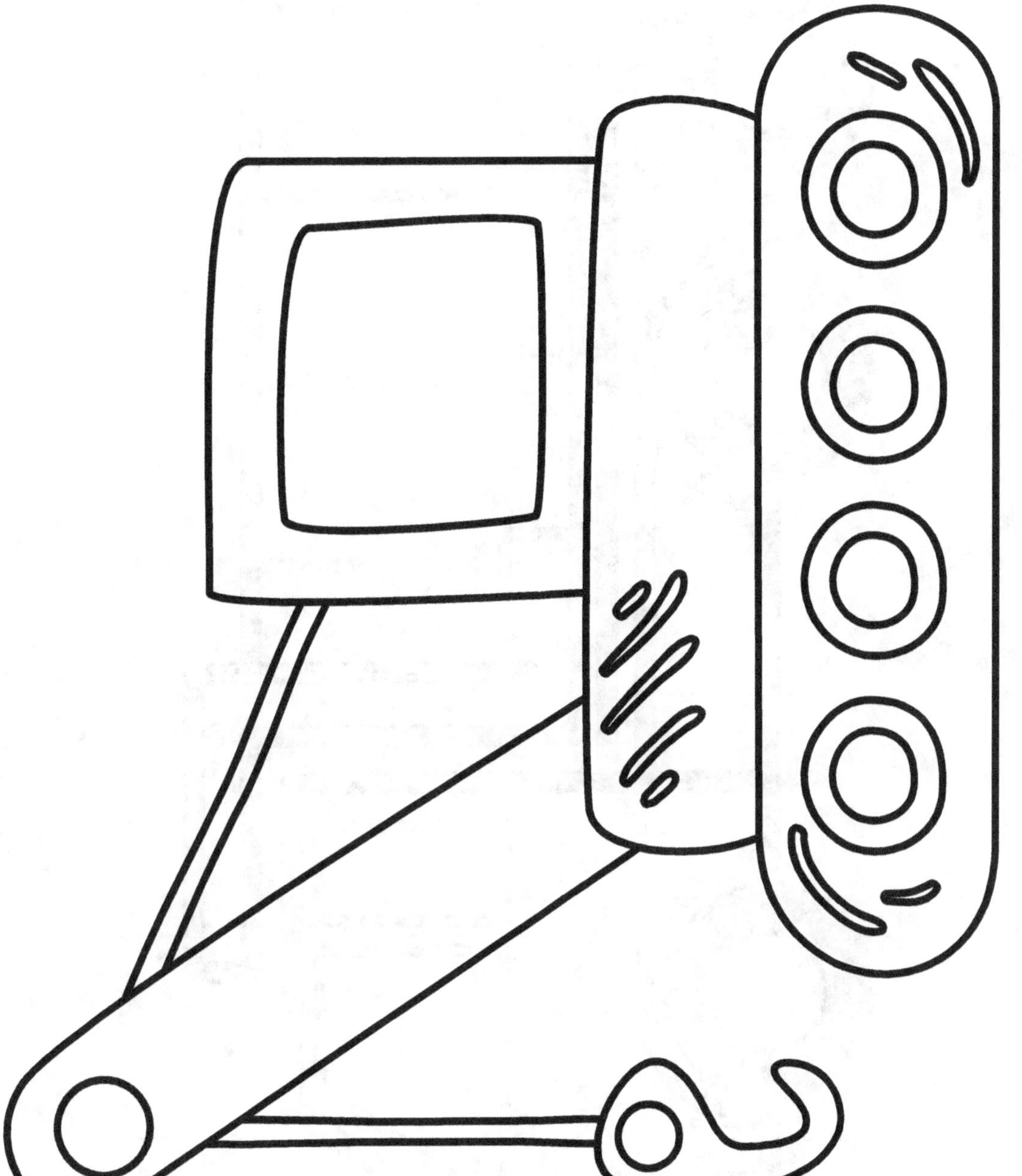

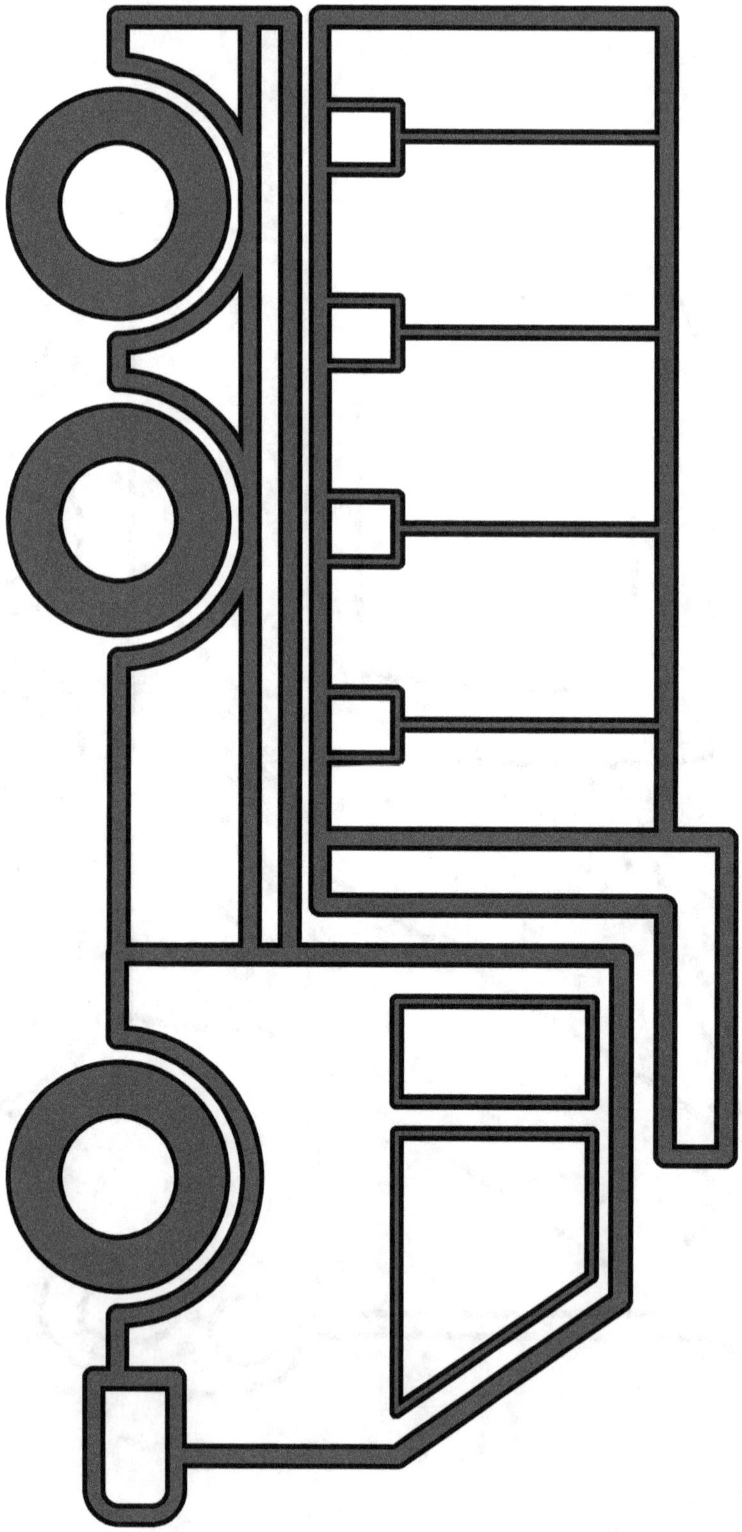

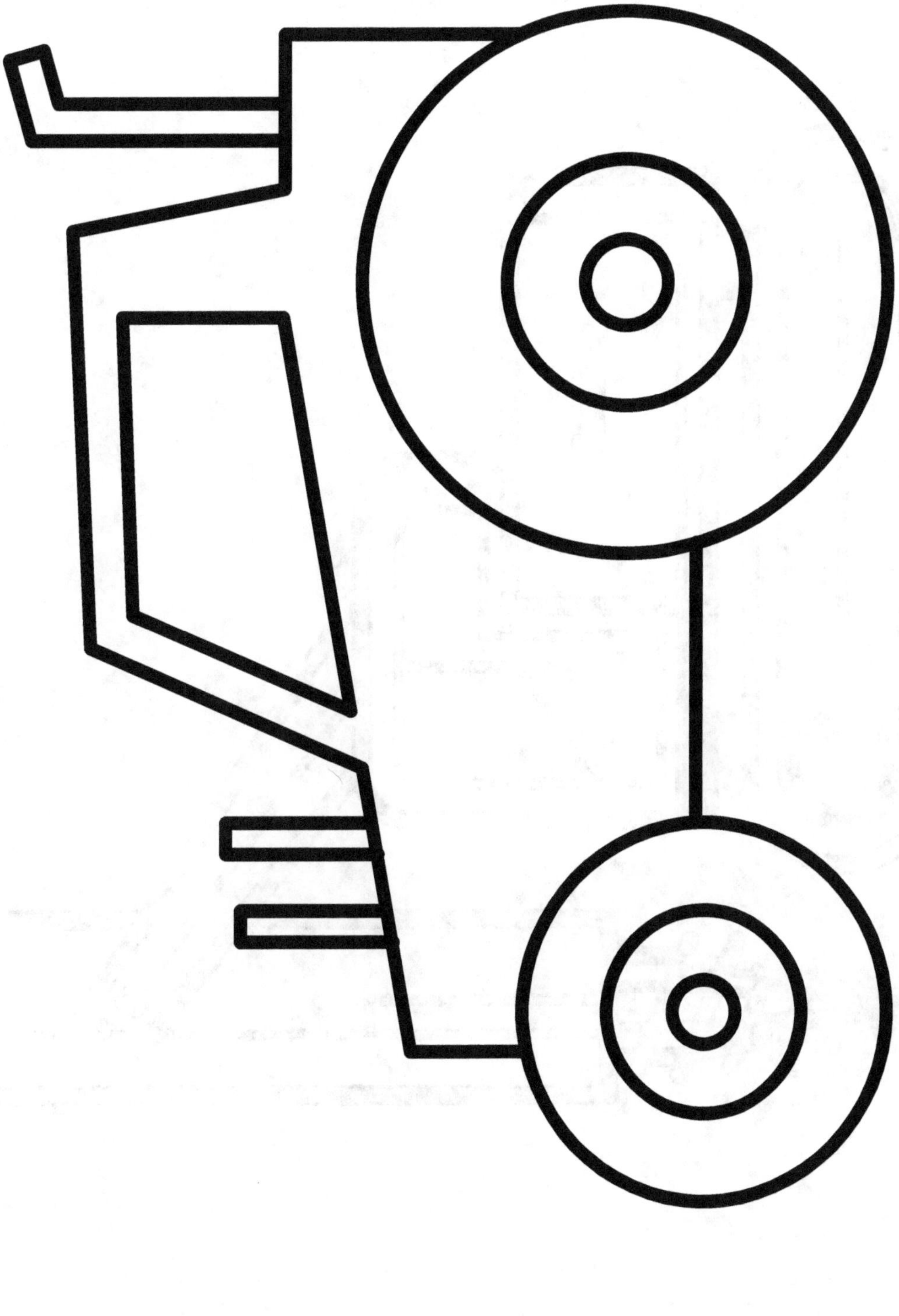

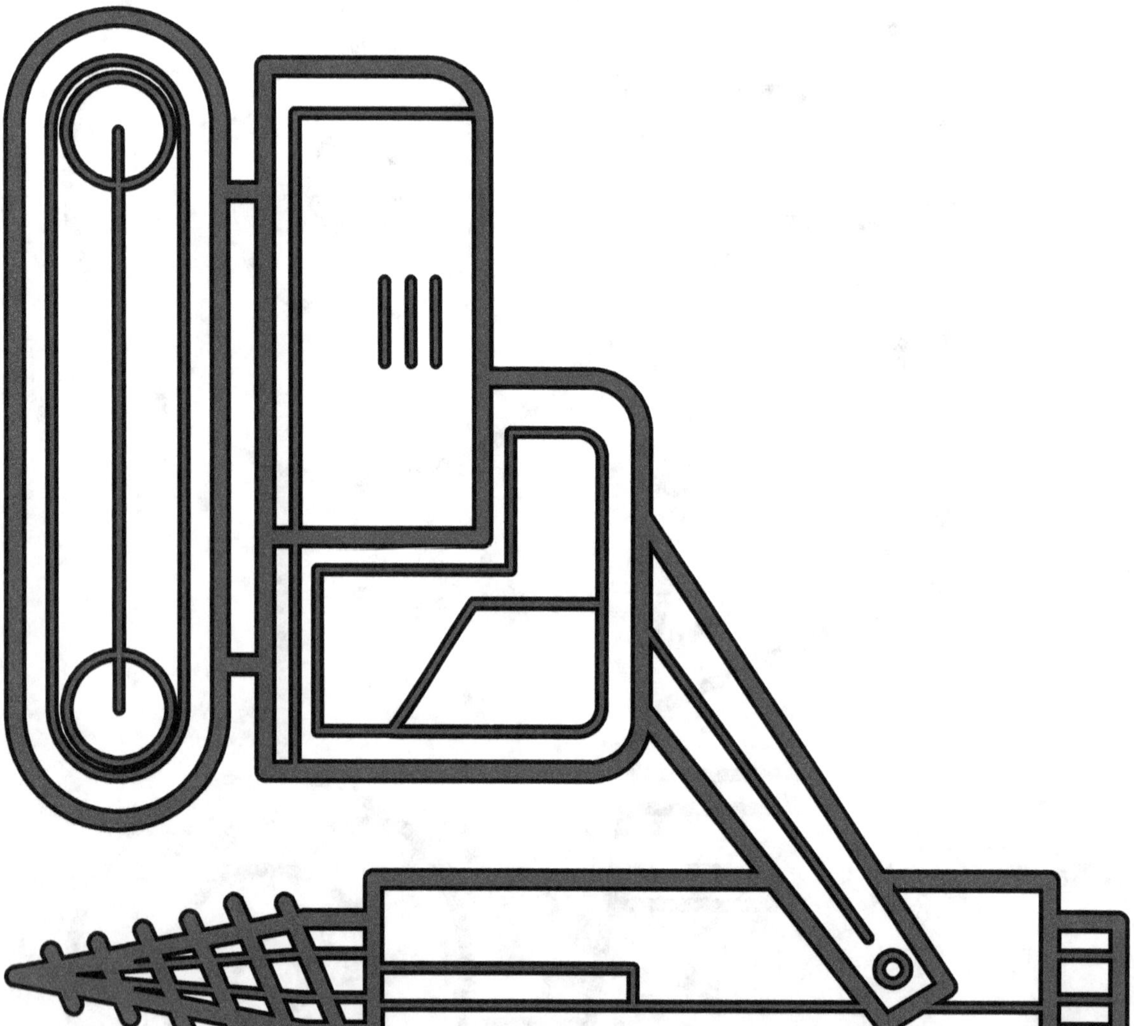

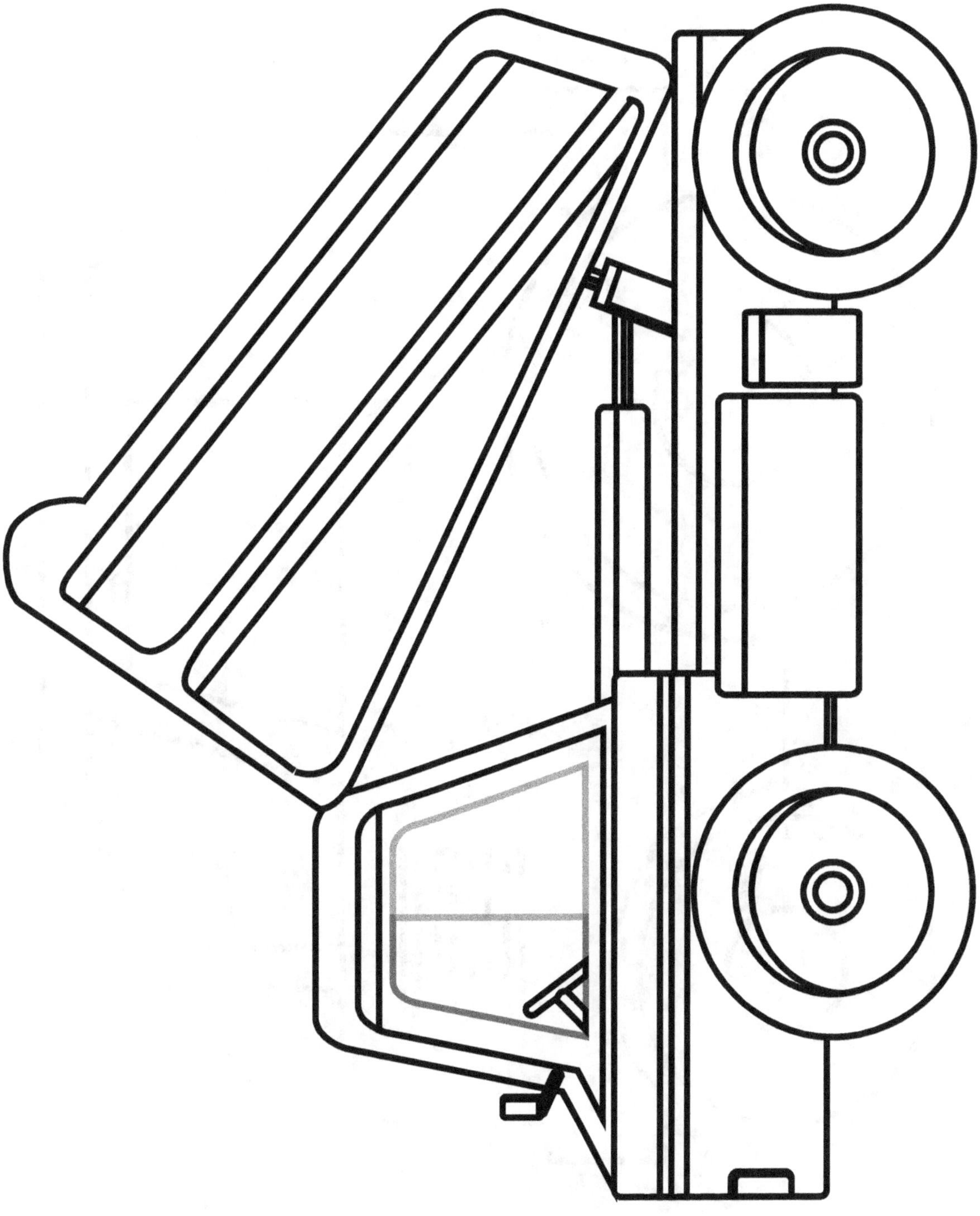

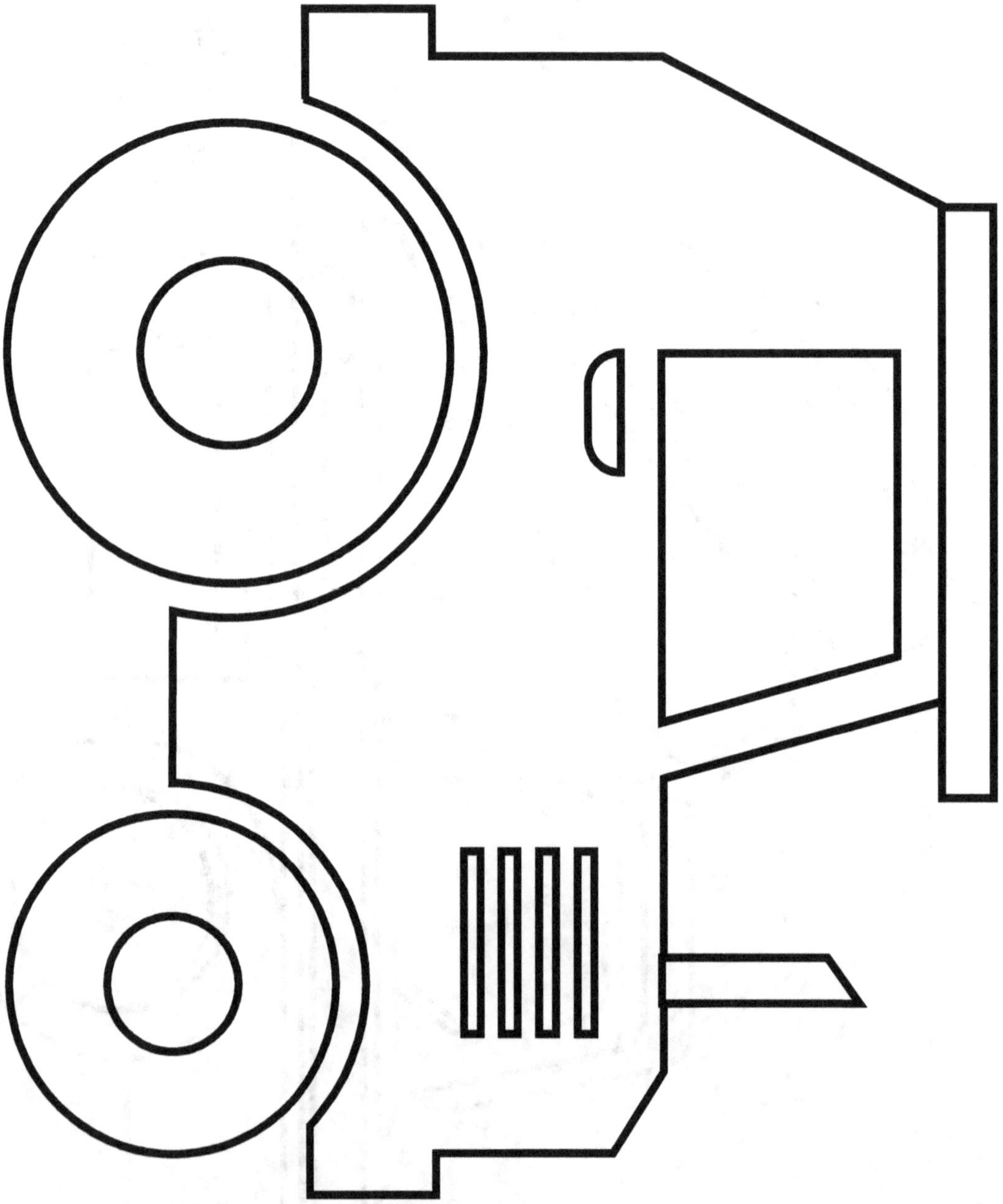

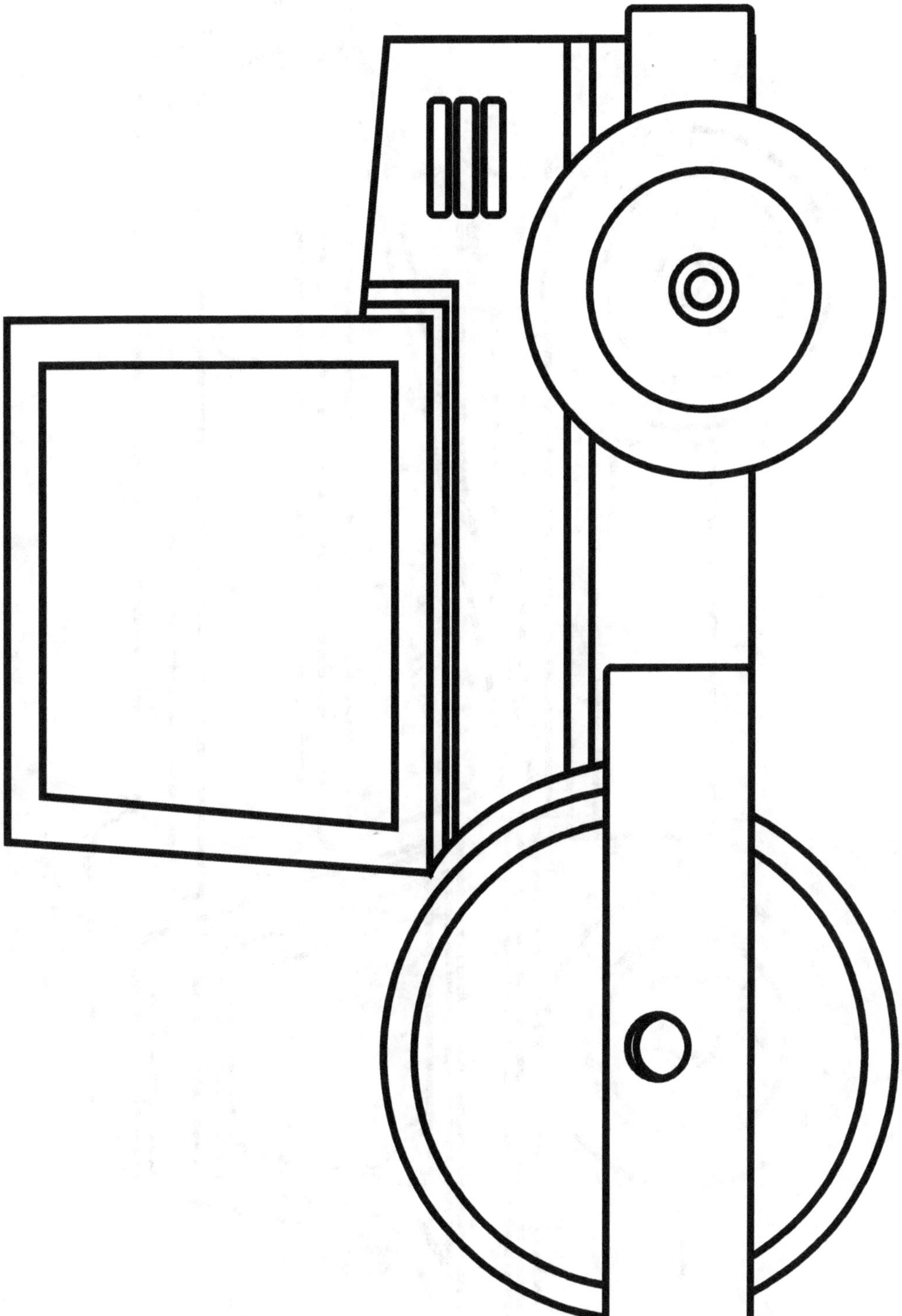

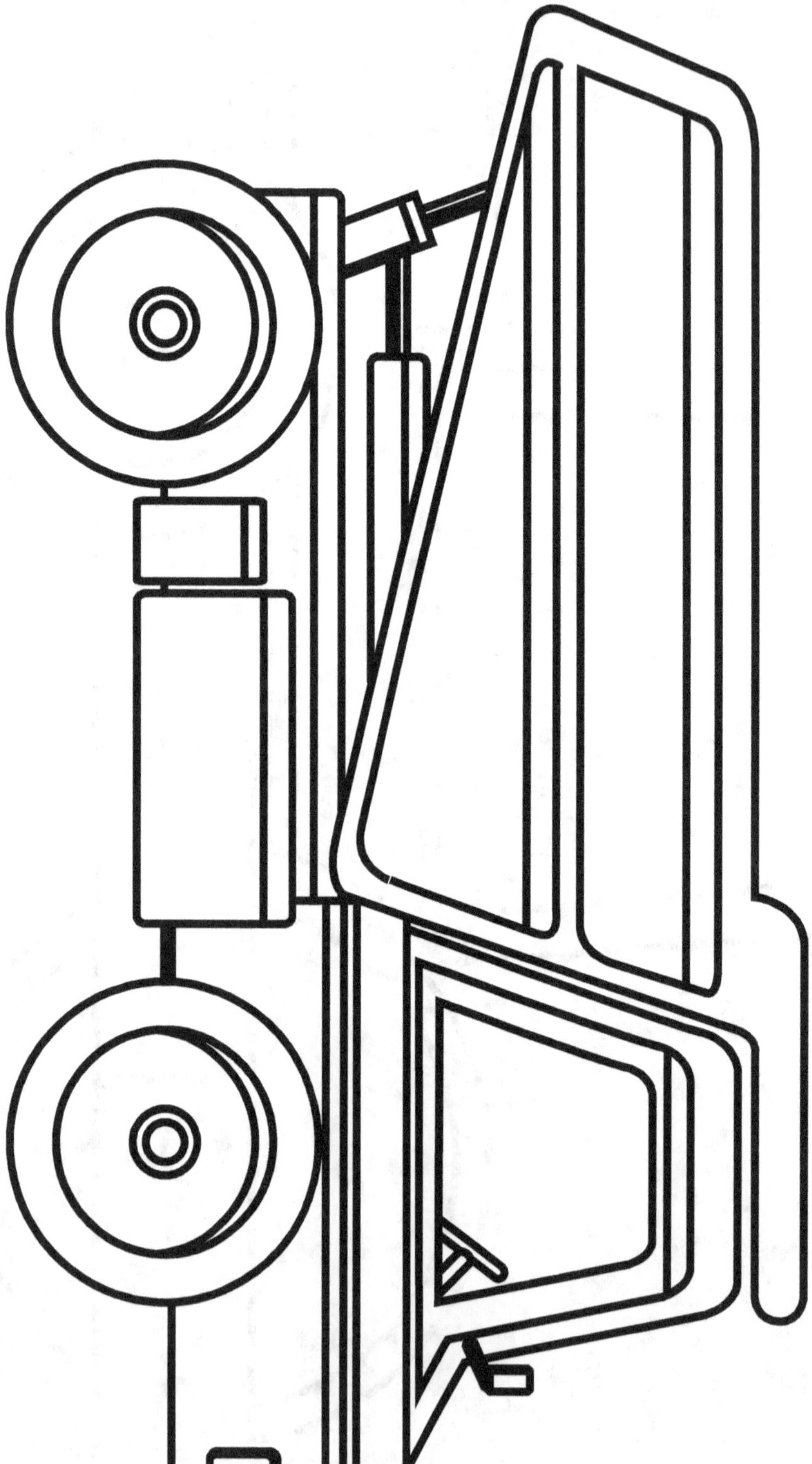

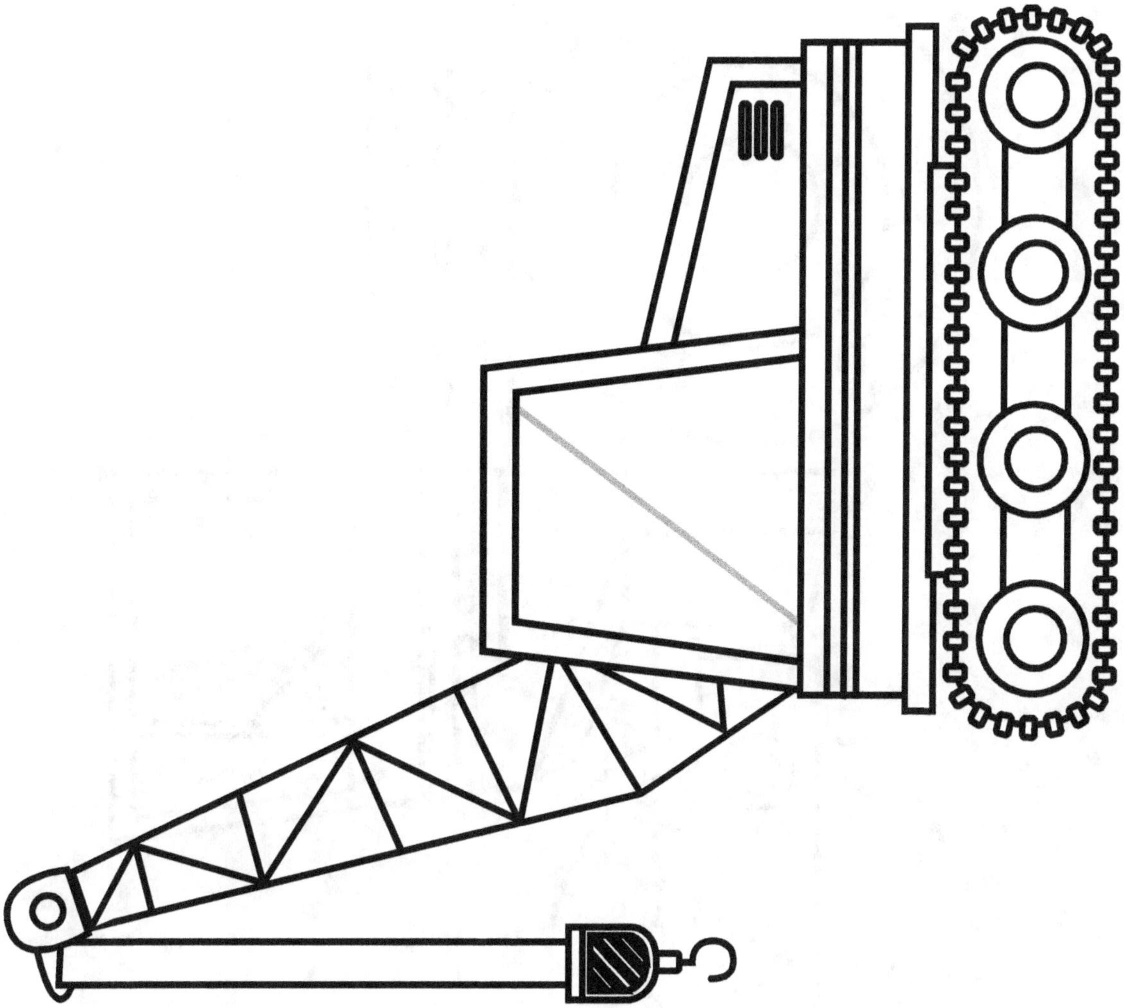

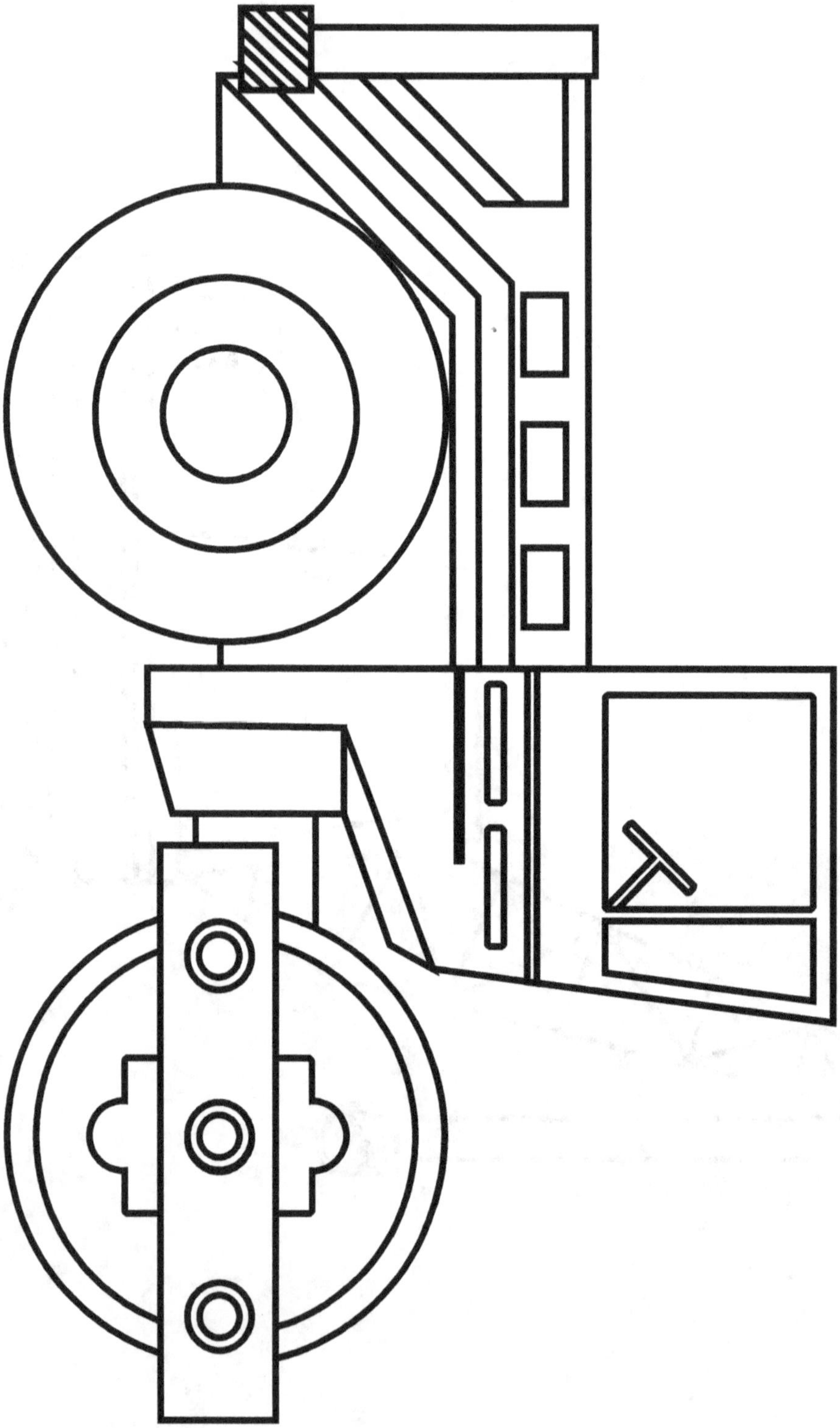

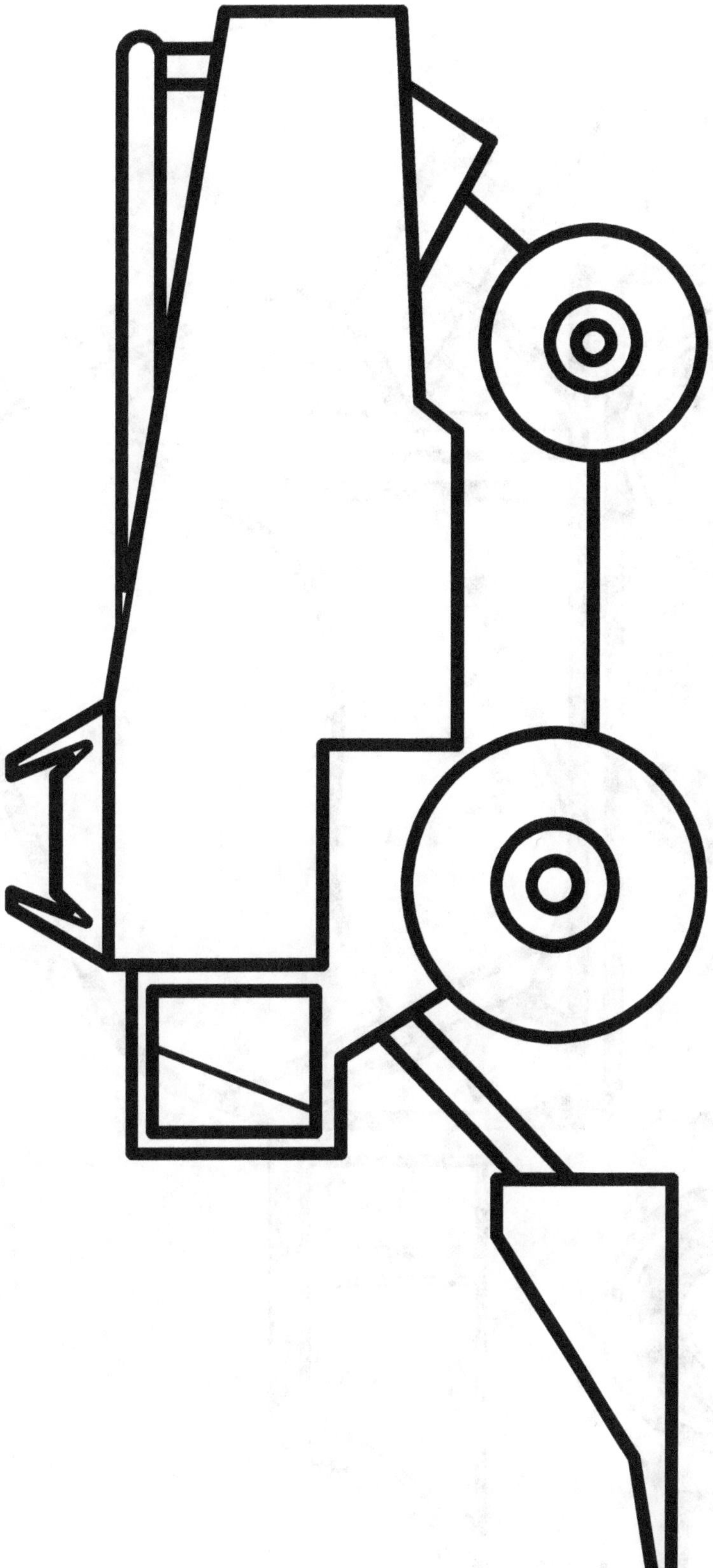

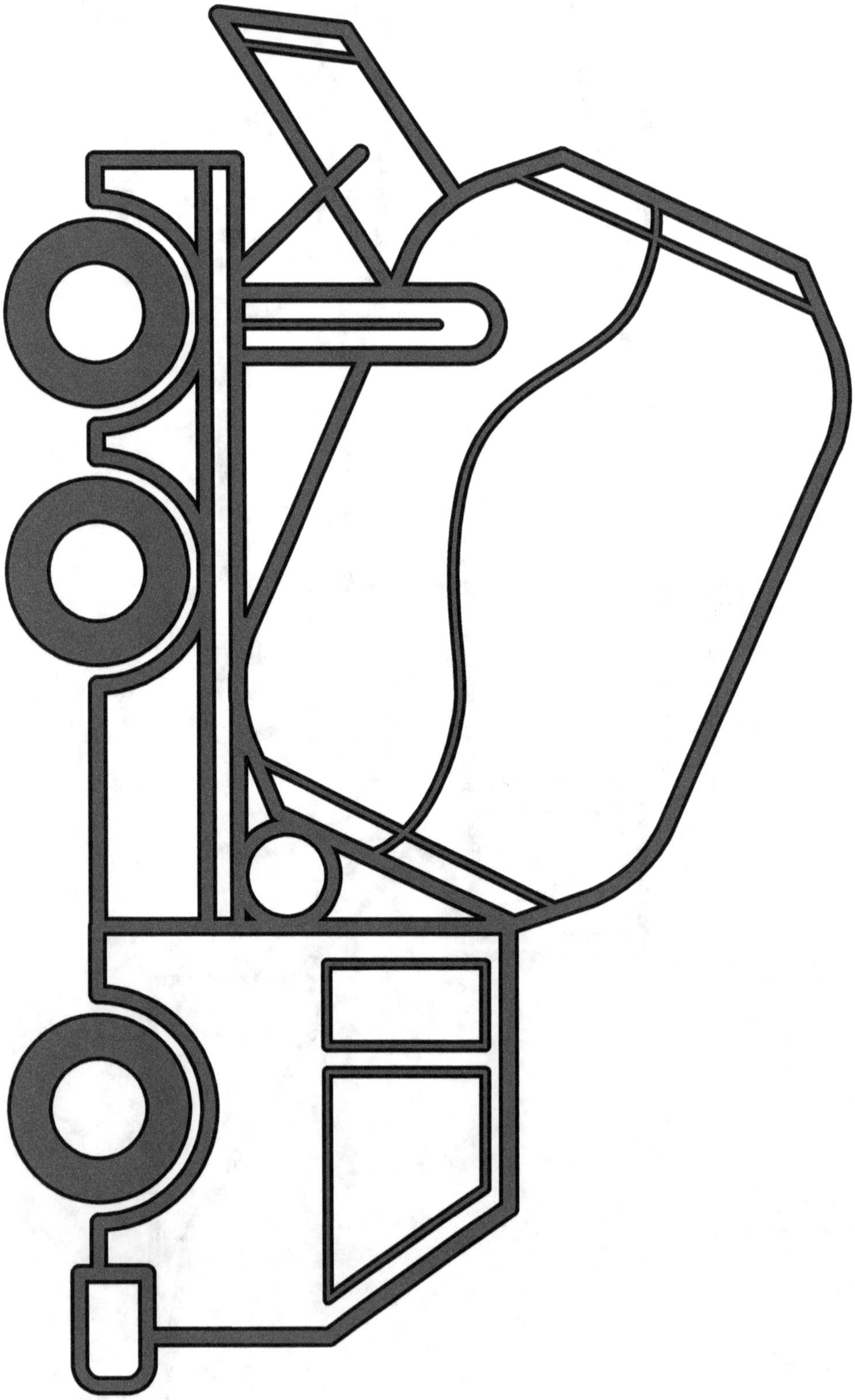

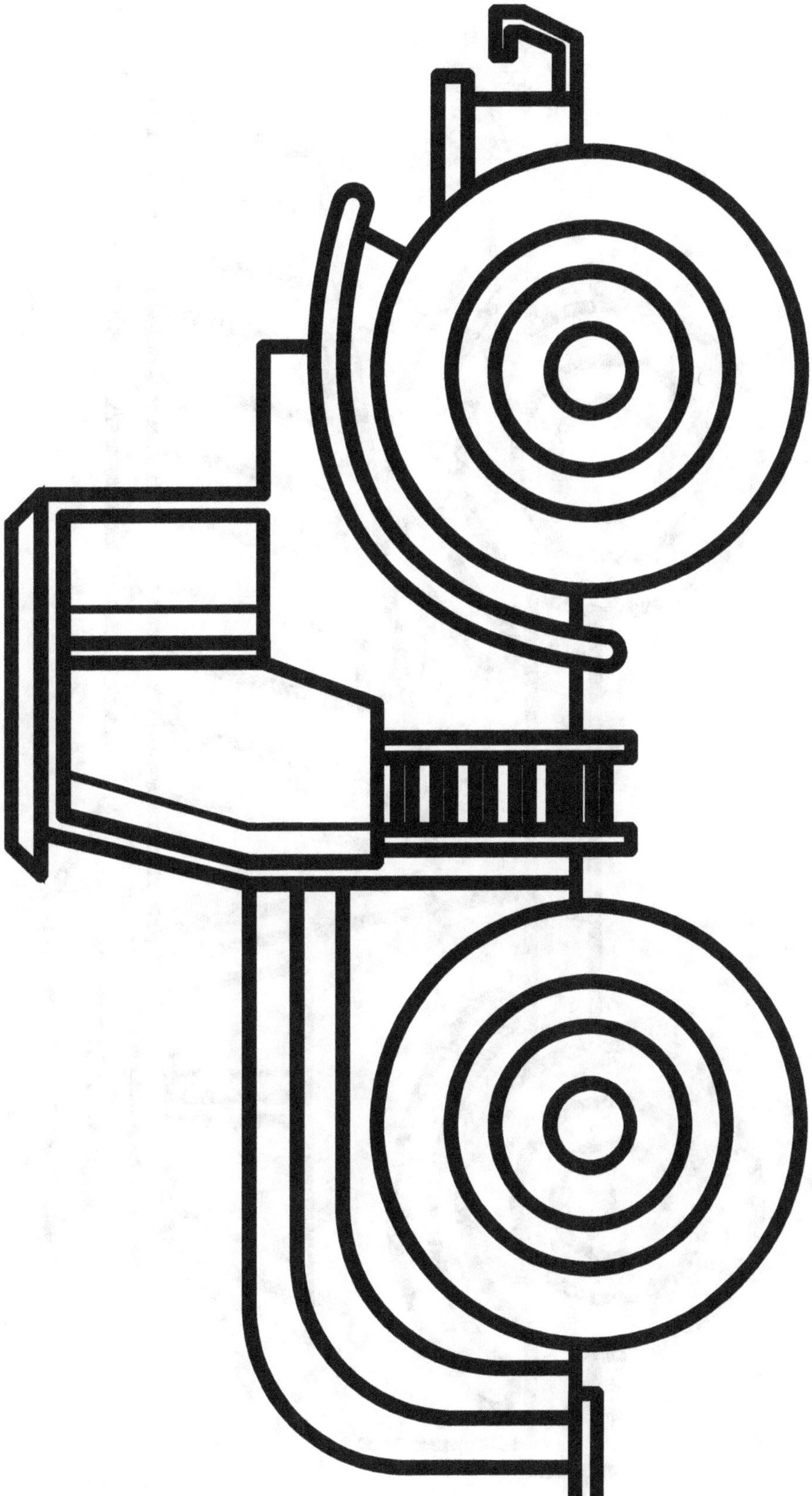

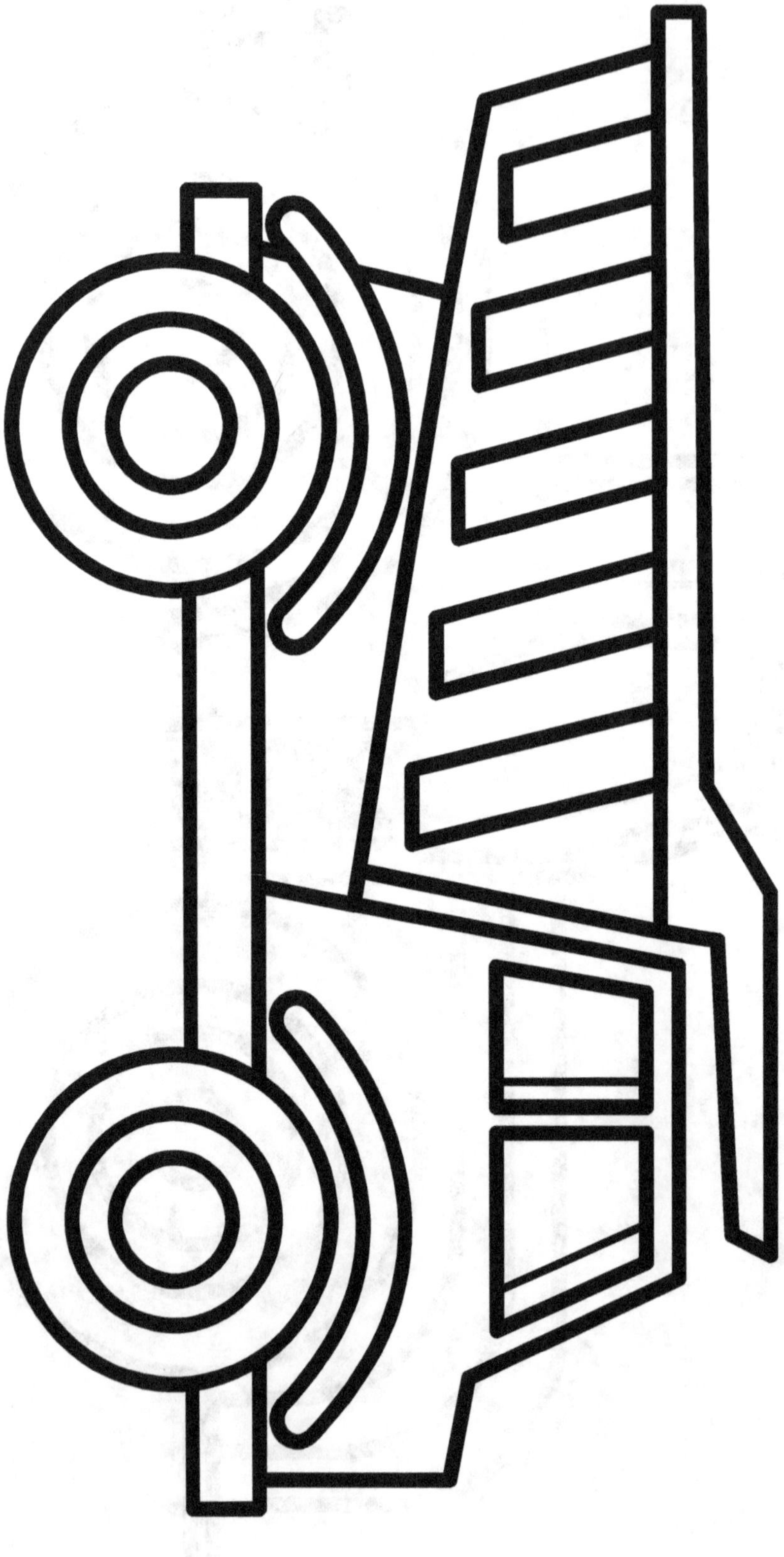

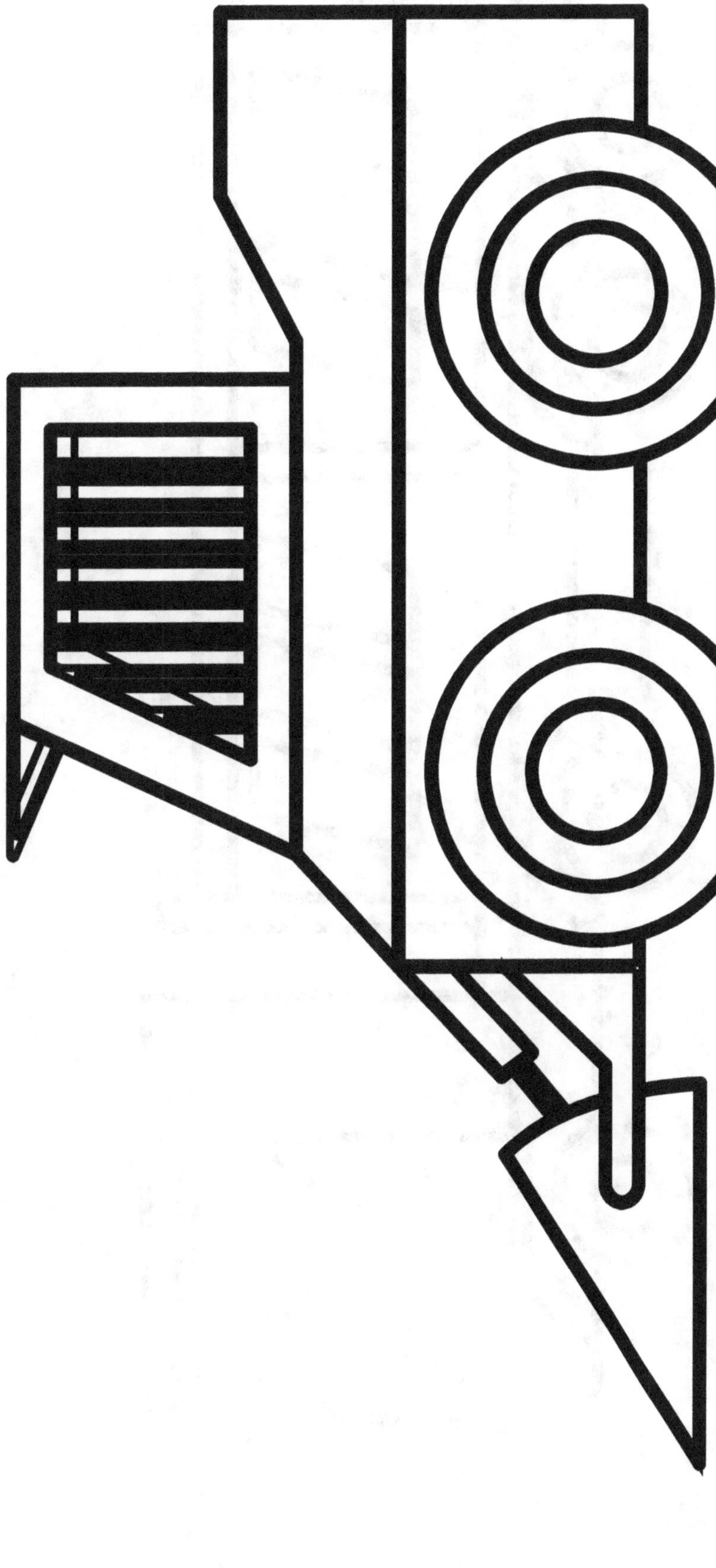

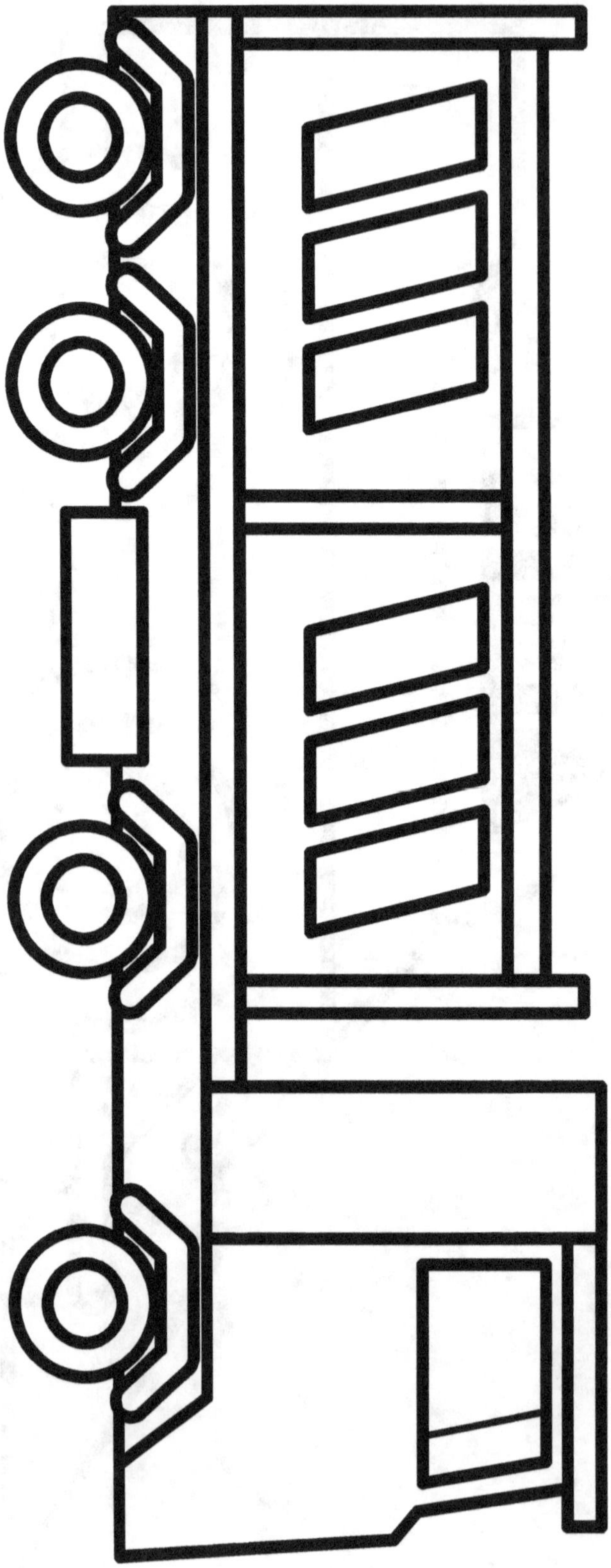

www.ingramcontent.com/pod-product-compliance
Lightning Source LLC
Chambersburg PA
CBHW081700220526
45466CB00009B/2835
* 9 7 9 8 5 5 3 7 7 6 8 0 0 *